Fact File 2012
Statistics brought alive!

3	Detailed contents	67	Financial issues	141	Sport & leisure
7	Alcohol, drugs & smoking	77	Food & drink	147	Travel & transport
		87	Health UK	157	War & conflict
15	Britain & its citizens	101	Health worldwide	167	Wider world
25	Education	111	Internet & media	183	Work
41	Environmental issues	119	Law & order	192	Index
53	Family & relationships	127	Population		

@nd online

Complete Issues
articles • opinions • statistics • contacts

Get instant online access to this book by logging on to:
www.completeissues.co.uk

User name: _____

Password: _____

...r details of **Complete Issues** ⟶

Editor: Christine Shepherd

CAREL PRESS
www.carelpress.com

Bracknell and Wokingham College

L0064409

The numbers behind the issues and controversies

The copiable book

The book has important statistics presented in an attractive and stimulating way. Readers will want to look at the figures and engage with the issues.

We've looked at hundreds of sources to select figures which are relevant to the curriculum and to the lives of young people. The book is ideal for reference or the sheer pleasure of browsing. It is also fully copiable – for research or classroom use.

Online

We are constantly expanding our online service. We have now integrated our three major publications – Fact File, Essential Articles and Key Organisations – in the Complete Issues Website. This allows you to search and browse all the books together, past and present editions, and to view and download those you've purchased. It is your one-stop source of facts, figures, opinions and further research. Go to: www.completeissues.co.uk

You can access all the statistics in Fact File as PDFs. We also provide you with the raw data and links to the sources. This makes it easy for you, staff or students to take research further and to create your own graphs using our data. You even have access to the archive of previous editions, giving you a wealth of statistics to use. Just typing a search term in www.completeissues.co.uk will produce all the pages you need - along with related articles and organisations.

Your purchase of the book entitles you to use this on one computer, however, buying a site licence makes the service and the material available to **all** students and staff at **all** times, even from home. **The site licence is included in the Complete Issues Package.**

If you do not yet have the other publications in the Complete Issues Package you can upgrade here: www.completeissues.co.uk

Activate your online access now at www.completeissues.co.uk/admin. Your admin login codes are on the covering letter – if anything isn't clear, please get in touch.

We have included a checklist poster of major topics and key words in the current Fact File and Essential Articles for you to display. You can record your log-in details there and on the front page of this book to make access to the online service quick and easy.

Unique features

Up-to-date: A new edition is published every year using the latest statistics.

Relevant: To the UK, its education system and the concerns of young people.

Organised: Statistics are grouped by theme, cross referenced, indexed and linked on the page to closely related statistics. Our online searches will find even more!

Attractive: Full colour and eye-catching with appealingly designed pages and great photos.

Easy to use: You don't have to worry about copyright issues as we've cleared these. Because you have both the book and online access you can use Fact File in different ways with different groups and in different locations. You can simultaneously use it in the library, in the classroom and at home.

Flexible: You can make paper copies, use a whiteboard or a computer. Different groups or individuals can be using different parts of the book at the same time. Having the raw data makes it even more adaptable.

Boosts library use: The posters provided free with each volume list the topics in Fact File and its sister publication Essential Articles and make it very easy to research issues. You can put one of your free posters in the library/LRC and one elsewhere – in the staff room, in a corridor, in a subject area. If you would like more copies of the poster just let us know.

Safe: Although we have included controversial topics and tackled difficult subjects, you can be confident that students are not going to encounter inappropriate material that an internet search might generate.

Accessible: Many of our statistics come from complex reports and are difficult to understand in their original form. The attractive and clear graphical presentation makes them accessible to young people – and the use of key words makes them easy to find.

Additional benefits: Subscribers to Essential Articles and Fact File are entitled to 10% discount on all our other products. They also receive occasional free posters to help promote library use and reading in general.

Published by Carel Press Ltd
4 Hewson St, Carlisle CA2 5AU
Tel +44 (0)1228 538928, Fax 591816
office@carelpress.co.uk
www.carelpress.com
© Carel Press

Research, design and editorial team:
Jack Gregory, Anne Louise Kershaw,
Debbie Maxwell, Christine A Shepherd, Chas White

Cover design: Anne Louise Kershaw
Photo of young Afghan girl: Tracing Tea / Shutterstock.com

Subscriptions: Ann Batey (Manager),
Brenda Hughes, Anne Maclagan

British Library Cataloguing in Publication Data
Fact file 2012 : essential statistics for today's key issues.
1. Great Britain--Statistics.
I. Shepherd, Christine A., 1951-
314.1
ISBN 978-1-905600-27-4

Printed by Finemark, Poland

FACT FILE 2012 CONTENTS

ALCOHOL, DRUGS & SMOKING

8 Under the influence
Age restrictions have not stopped most young people from having an alcoholic drink and many set out simply to get drunk

10 On a downer
Drug use among 11-15 year olds has declined since 2001

12 Young smokers
Young people are more likely to smoke if their family and friends do

14 Danger, danger
What habits do Brits perceive as most dangerous...and are they right?

BRITAIN AND ITS CITIZENS

16 Typically British
The characteristics people associate with being British

17 Community spirit
Most people think their area is a place where people from different backgrounds get along well

18 Integrating immigrants
How does the UK match up to other countries in helping newcomers to live, work and participate in society?

20 Equals
Most people believe that household tasks should be shared equally between men and women – but the reality is different

22 Generation rent
From a nation of home owners we are becoming a nation of renters

24 Who are you?
What would you leave for future generations to learn about you and your life?

EDUCATION

26 Only average
What is a typical secondary school?

28 Teacher talk
Teachers say they love their job, but it's getting harder

30 Classroom crackdown
Parents and pupils agree that there should be more discipline - but don't agree on the methods

32 Forced out
Bullying is a problem for many children – and for some it means missing out on education

34 True faith?
60% of people think group worship should not be enforced in schools

36 Reading progress
Many young people in the UK don't enjoy reading – how much does this matter?

38 Debt sentence
The recession has increased the strain of university costs and parents are finding it harder to support their child financially

40 Degree of debt
UK students entering higher education in 2011/12 should expect to owe around £26,100 on graduation

ENVIRONMENTAL ISSUES

42 Good behaviour
Shoppers are making more 'green' choices than a decade ago

44 Stop the drop
Over 2.5 million pieces of litter are dropped on UK streets every day and almost half of us admit to dropping litter at some time

46 Beachwatch
Beach litter has almost doubled over the last 15 years

48 Hidden waters
Fresh water is a scarce resource and demand is growing. We need to look at our personal 'water footprint'

50 Nuclear future?
Nuclear power supplies around 14% of the world's electricity – but is it safe?

52 Life on earth
We don't yet know the number of species on Earth – but we know some are disappearing even before scientists have classified them

23.6% of year 9 pupils state bullying as a reason for absence from school

page 33

6.9% of children have been physically attacked by an adult during their childhood

page 56

FAMILY & RELATIONSHIPS

54 Family friendly
The best places to bring up children: safe, leafy and with good schools

56 Safe house
'No child should have to live in fear or on edge in their own home' – but many do

58 Could you tell?
How many of us could spot the signs of child sexual exploitation?

60 Someone to talk to
Most children and young people have some aspect of their lives they worry about ... but most have relationships in their lives which support them

62 Under pressure
The issues that parents think children might face today – from testing in school to whether they are happy

63 Finding families
Only 60 babies in care were adopted last year ... is the process too slow and too cautious?

64 Happy anniversary
The divorce rate has fallen to its lowest since 1974

66 Man of the house
How happy are couples with their roles within the family?

FINANCIAL ISSUES

68 Pocket money
What is the right amount of pocket money?

70 100% giving
What made donors to charity open their wallets in 2011?

72 In it to win it
Nearly three quarters of adults in Britain gamble – and for some it becomes a problem

74 Deep in debt
Personal debts in Britain are so high that we owe more than we earn!

75 Debt hotspots
People seeking help had an average debt of more than £19,000, but there are large differences in debt between different regions in the UK

76 Struggling to save
6 million people in Britain have no savings at all

FOOD & DRINK

78 Ethical eating
We have concerns about ethical eating, yet we do not act on them

80 Organic market
Although shoppers would like to buy organic food, they are also feeling the economic pinch

82 Time to eat
Most parents were happy with their child's school meal arrangements but they wanted to see some improvements

84 Calorie conscious
Over half of us do not know how many calories we are consuming when we eat out – and our guesses fall short of the reality

86 Keep calm and bake
Whether it's cupcakes or Cordon Bleu, home baking has boomed during the recession

HEALTH UK

88 Eating disorders
Young women aged between 10 and 24 are the group most frequently admitted to hospital for an eating disorder

90 Visible difference
Despite the recession, the public's interest in cosmetic surgery was still strong in 2010

92 Sting in the tale
It is hard to prevent insect stings but why aren't we reducing the number of dog bites?

94 Common cancers
An estimated 39% of 12 of the most common cancers in the UK could be prevented

96 HIV in the UK
UK-acquired HIV has nearly doubled over the past decade

98 TB in the UK
Tuberculosis cases have risen in the UK to over 9,000 – the highest number for nearly 30 years

100 Malaria in the UK
Malaria is a potentially deadly disease but is almost completely preventable

HEALTH WORLDWIDE

102 The big killers: Malaria
About 3.3 billion people – half of the world's population – are at risk of malaria

104 The big killers: Cancer
There are an estimated 12.7 million cancer cases around the world every year. By 2030 there could be 26 million cases

106 The big killers: TB
Worldwide, an estimated 1.7 million people died of TB and there were 9.4 million new cases, mainly in Asia and Africa

108 Living with HIV
There are around 30.8 million adults and 2.5 million children living with HIV – but the world is beginning to reverse its spread

110 Dying of AIDS
There are about 15 million people living with HIV in low- and middle-income countries who need treatment today

INTERNET & MEDIA

112 Basic needs
One in three young people feel that internet access is as vital as air, food and water

114 Generation app
People's relationships with their mobile phones have changed over recent years

116 Being sociable
Users are most likely to use social networks for interacting and keeping up to date with friends. The average Facebook user has 130 friends

118 Who's online?
Internet users in Europe – only the Netherlands has a higher percentage of users than the UK

LAW & ORDER

120 I predict a riot
Who was in court after the August 2011 riots... and what happened to them?

122 Locked up
More than 10.1 million people are held in prisons throughout the world

124 Who's inside?
Compared to the general population, prisoners are five times as likely to have run away from home as a child and more than ten times as likely to have been in care

126 Prison population
The number of prisoners has soared

POPULATION

128 Population clock
The global population rose to 6.9 billion in 2010, with nearly all of that growth in the world's developing countries

130 Future generation
There are 1.2 billion young people in the world – 18% of the world's population

132 Shape of things to come?
The population of developed countries is ageing and there is little growth. In developing countries the population is young and is growing

134 Full stop?
World population has reached 7 billion. Will it continue to increase or will we see 'zero population growth'?

136 Crowded planet
Do we have room for our growing population?

137 Urban sprawl
An estimated 59% of the world's population will live in urban areas by 2030

138 Population pyramid
The gender, age and marital status of the population in England and Wales

140 Born and bred
Where people now living in the UK were born

SPORT & LEISURE

142 'To do' list
Heritage, sport and shopping are top attractions for visitors to Britain

144 Running out of time?
Although 53% of women say they want to do more sport, far fewer women than men are getting sporty

146 Support for sport
Attitudes towards the 2012 Olympic Games

World population is expected to reach between 9.15 & 9.51 billion by 2050

page 134

TRAVEL & TRANSPORT

148 Falling fatalities
Over the course of a decade, road deaths have reduced dramatically in high income countries. But 90% of road deaths in the world occur in low and middle income countries

150 Cycle of destruction
Despite the reduction in the number of overall road deaths, there was a significant rise in motorcycle deaths in many countries

152 Travel trends
The recession continued to affect where Brits go for their holidays...

154 Wish you were here?
Foreign Office staff handled 19,228 serious cases for Brits abroad in 2010 – but there's a limit to the help they can give

156 Give mums a break
Mums end up being just as busy on holiday as they are when they're at home

WAR & CONFLICT

158 Forced to flee
People can be refugees even within their own country – and the number of these displaced people is continuing to rise

160 Barriers to education
Millennium Development Goal 2 was to make sure every child had at least primary education...but we are not likely to achieve this – especially in countries affected by conflict

162 Dangerous waters
Off the coast of Somalia – and now on land – heavily armed pirates are capturing vessels and people to hold to ransom

164 The cost of peace
United Nations peacekeeping staff help countries torn by conflict to create conditions for lasting peace – but sometimes the cost is their own lives

166 War & peace
For the third year running the world is less peaceful

WIDER WORLD

168 Promises, promises
In 2010, development aid to sub-Saharan Africa was the highest on record but still fell short of the commitments made in 2005

170 Making progress? Safe drinking water
The world is on track to meet the Millennium Development Goal on drinking water

172 Making progress? Sanitation
The world is likely to miss the Millennium Development Goal on sanitation – a billion people will still be without this basic necessity by 2015

174 Worlds apart
Nordic countries continue to lead the way towards gender equality, but no country has yet achieved it

176 Child brides
"Child marriage denies girls their childhood, deprives them of an education and robs them of their innocence" – yet it is common in some countries

178 Child birth
About 16 million adolescent girls aged 15-19 give birth each year. This is more than 10% of all births worldwide

180 Missing midwives
Every year, 48 million women give birth without someone with the right skills. More than 2 million women give birth completely alone

182 AIDS orphans
Even though HIV worldwide has declined and more people have access to treatment, the total number of children who have lost their parents due to HIV has not gone down

WORK

184 Workless
The number of households with no-one in work has declined, but there are more people who have NEVER worked

186 Class of 2011
Graduates are scrambling for jobs

188 Missing women
More women than ever are working, but they are not making it to the top

190 Who's busiest?
On average, people spend about a third of their time in paid or unpaid work. But the proportion is very different between countries and between genders

192 Index

By the end of 2009, the AIDS epidemic had left behind 16.6 million orphans

page 182

Alcohol, drugs & smoking

Under the influence

Lots of young people have had an alcoholic drink despite age restrictions

5,700 students in Year 9 and Year 11 in England were asked about their drinking habits and influences

Most young people were **aged 11 and over** when they had their **first drink**, most commonly around 12 to 13.

Around **75%** of each year group said they were **with an adult** when they first drank alcohol – celebrating a **special occasion** such as a family or religious event.

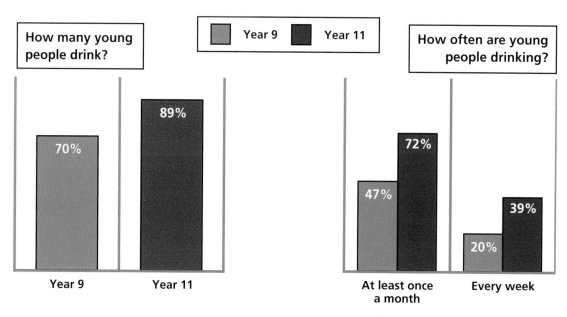

How many young people drink?

Year 9 | Year 11

Year 9: 70%
Year 11: 89%

How often are young people drinking?

At least once a month — Year 9: 47%, Year 11: 72%
Every week — Year 9: 20%, Year 11: 39%

For those who **hadn't** had a drink, this was mainly due to **lack of interest** in alcohol.

27% of Year 9 students and 49% of Year 11 students who drink alcohol had a drink the **previous week**.

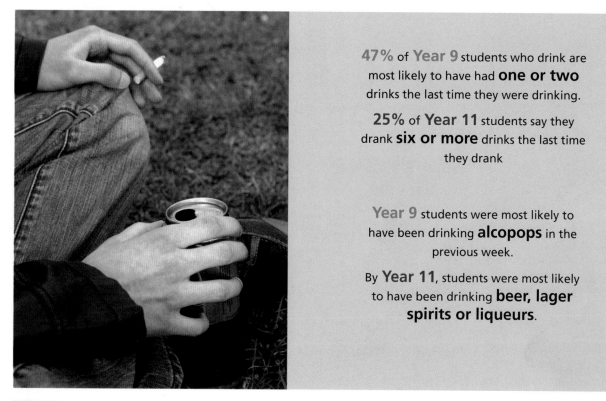

47% of Year 9 students who drink are most likely to have had **one or two** drinks the last time they were drinking.

25% of Year 11 students say they drank **six or more** drinks the last time they drank

Year 9 students were most likely to have been drinking **alcopops** in the previous week.

By Year 11, students were most likely to have been drinking **beer, lager spirits or liqueurs**.

Who are they drinking with?

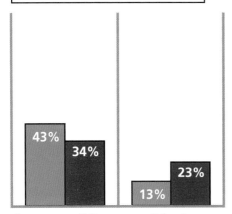

| 43% | 34% | | 13% | 23% |
| Parents or siblings | | | Friends | |

Whilst both year groups are most likely to have been drinking at home the last time they drank, this reduces as young people get older.

In many cases, getting drunk was intentional.

54% of Year 9 students who have had an alcoholic drink said they have been drunk. Around the same proportions said this has happened **only once** as said they had been drunk **more than once.**

By Year 11, **79%** of students have been drunk, **52%** saying they had been drunk more than once.

Number of students who have been drunk who said that they and their friends drink to get drunk at least once a month

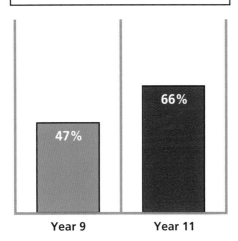

| 47% | 66% |
| Year 9 | Year 11 |

Source: Young people, alcohol and influences: A study of young people and their relationship with alcohol, Ipsos Mori for Joseph Rowntree Foundation www.jrf.org.uk

Peer influence:

The more of their friends they thought were drinking, the more likely young people were to have been drinking alcohol the previous week.

Friends' drinking also influenced the **amount** young people drink.

Family influence:

Parents strongly influence young people's alcohol-related behaviour through supervision and monitoring. Seeing family members drinking and perceptions of drunkenness among family members in the home can make this kind of drinking appear normal.

Attitudes:

Young people are more likely to behave in certain ways with alcohol if they believe it is acceptable to act that way.

If they think that drinking will be fun and make them happy, this increases the likelihood of them drinking.

Fear of not being able to stop drinking or being sick, decreases the likelihood.

SEE ALSO:
Let's be realistic about teen drinking, p14, Essential Articles 13
Mother's ruin, p16, Essential Articles 13
Road to recovery? p8, Fact File 2011
www.completeissues.co.uk

On a downer

Drug use among 11-15 year olds has declined since 2001

In 2010, 18% of pupils reported that they had ever taken drugs. 12% said they had taken drugs in the last year.

Cannabis was the most widely used drug;

8.2% of pupils reported taking it in the last year.

Older pupils were more likely to have taken drugs.

	11 year olds	15 year olds
Ever taken drugs	9%	32%
In last year	5%	25%
In last month	2%	14%

Proportion of pupils who took drugs in the last month, last year and ever: 2001-2010

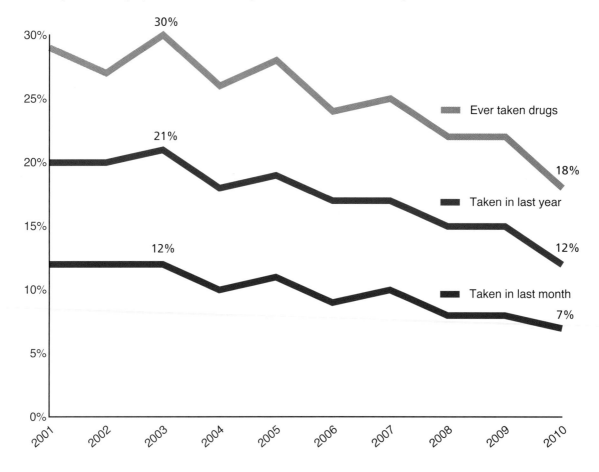

Proportion of pupils who have taken individual drugs

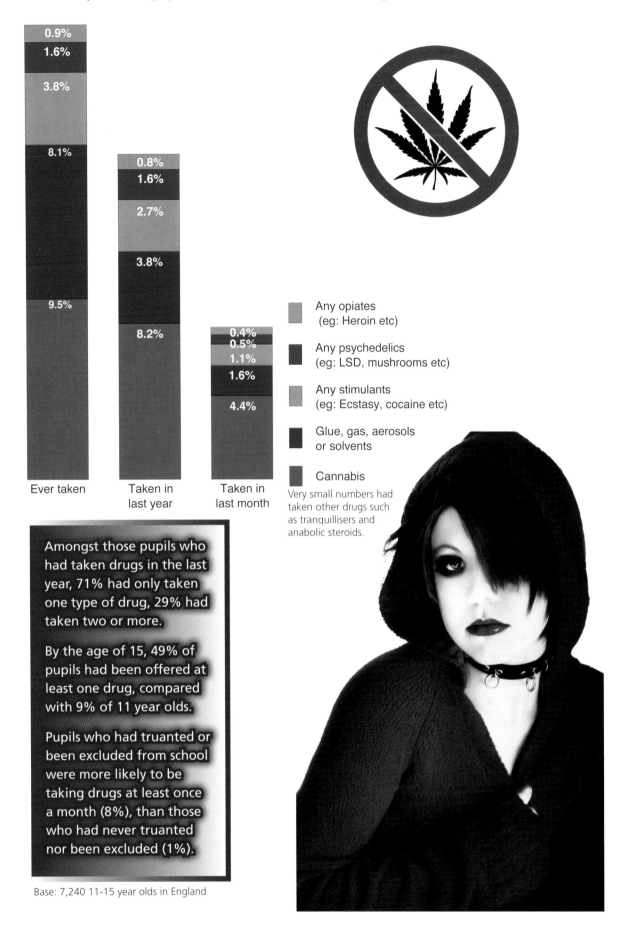

Ever taken
- 0.9%
- 1.6%
- 3.8%
- 8.1%
- 9.5%

Taken in last year
- 0.8%
- 1.6%
- 2.7%
- 3.8%
- 8.2%

Taken in last month
- 0.4%
- 0.5%
- 1.1%
- 1.6%
- 4.4%

Legend:
- Any opiates (eg: Heroin etc)
- Any psychedelics (eg: LSD, mushrooms etc)
- Any stimulants (eg: Ecstasy, cocaine etc)
- Glue, gas, aerosols or solvents
- Cannabis

Very small numbers had taken other drugs such as tranquillisers and anabolic steroids.

Amongst those pupils who had taken drugs in the last year, 71% had only taken one type of drug, 29% had taken two or more.

By the age of 15, 49% of pupils had been offered at least one drug, compared with 9% of 11 year olds.

Pupils who had truanted or been excluded from school were more likely to be taking drugs at least once a month (8%), than those who had never truanted nor been excluded (1%).

Base: 7,240 11-15 year olds in England

Source: Smoking, drinking and drug use among young people in England in 2010, NHS © 2011 Health and Social Care Information Centre
www.dh.gov.uk

SEE ALSO:
Road to recovery? p8, Fact File 2011
www.completeissues.co.uk

Young smokers

Young people are more likely to smoke if their family and friends do

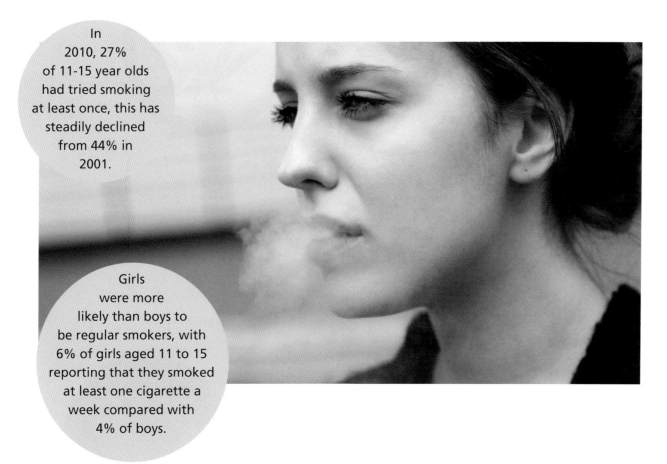

In 2010, 27% of 11-15 year olds had tried smoking at least once, this has steadily declined from 44% in 2001.

Girls were more likely than boys to be regular smokers, with 6% of girls aged 11 to 15 reporting that they smoked at least one cigarette a week compared with 4% of boys.

Percentage of pupils who smoke

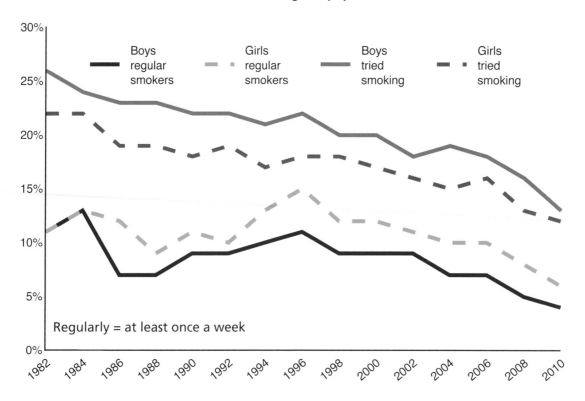

Boys regular smokers
Girls regular smokers
Boys tried smoking
Girls tried smoking

Regularly = at least once a week

The proportion of pupils who had ever smoked increased with age: 4% of 11 year olds compared with 49% of 15 year olds. Less than 0.5% of 11 year olds said that they smoked at least one cigarette a week, but this increased to 12% amongst 15 year olds.

Most people knew someone who smoked cigarettes, and this was more likely to be a family member (67%) than a friend (54%). Among family members, 33% of pupils reported that a parent or guardian smoked, 13% that a brother or sister smoked and 51% that another relative was a smoker.

Percentage of pupils who smoke by number of smokers pupil lives with

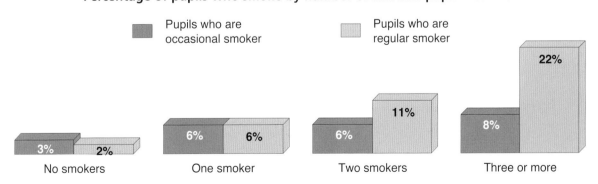

Pupils who are occasional smoker

Pupils who are regular smoker

No smokers	One smoker	Two smokers	Three or more
3% 2%	6% 6%	6% 11%	8% 22%

Base: 7,252 young people aged 11-15

Source: Smoking, drinking and drug use among young people in England in 2010, NHS © 2011 Health & social care information centre
www.ic.nhs.uk

SEE ALSO:
www.completeissues.co.uk

Danger, danger

What habits do Brits perceive as most dangerous... and are they right?

How **safe** or **dangerous** do you think the following activities are:

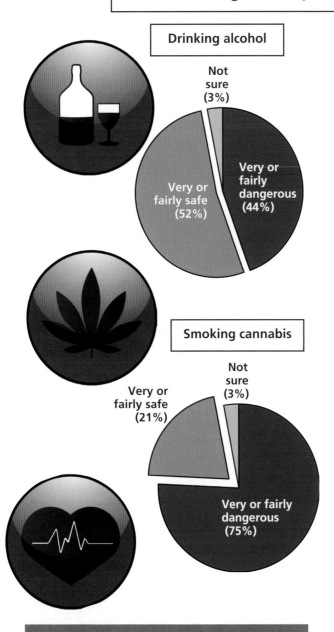

Drinking alcohol

Not sure (3%)

Very or fairly safe (52%)

Very or fairly dangerous (44%)

Smoking cigarettes

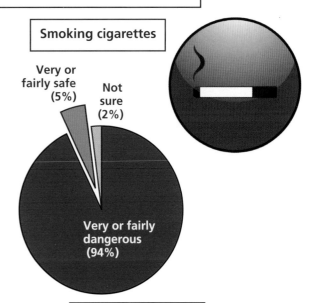

Very or fairly safe (5%)

Not sure (2%)

Very or fairly dangerous (94%)

Smoking cannabis

Not sure (3%)

Very or fairly safe (21%)

Very or fairly dangerous (75%)

Taking Ecstasy

Very or fairly safe (10%)

Not sure (2%)

Very or fairly dangerous (88%)

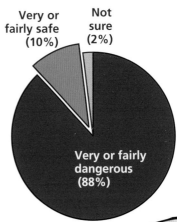

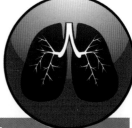

Alcohol & drugs

Drinking alcohol was thought to be the safest activity while taking Ecstasy was seen as one of the most dangerous. But the statistics suggest a different story as figures from the US and the UK report only **7** ecstasy-related deaths per million users of the drug (many of these due to mixing the drug with alcohol) in comparison to **625** alcohol-related deaths per million drinkers that occur each year.

Cigarettes

British opinion was far more in line with the official statistics when it came to the dangers of smoking which causes the deaths of about **106,000** people in the UK each year.

Base: 1,940 GB adults

Source: YouGov © 2011
www.yougov.com

SEE ALSO:
Where's the harm? p54, Essential Articles 14
www.completeissues.co.uk

Britain & its citizens

Typically British

What makes us feel British?

When asked what being 'British' meant, the top characteristics that people associate with the term include:

Characteristic	Percentage
Drinking tea	60%
Talking about the weather	59%
Good at queuing	47%
Speaking English when abroad	42%
Keeping a stiff upper lip	40%
Supportive of the Royal Family	34%
Being loyal to friends and family	32%
Liking to moan	30%
Hard working	29%
Getting drunk abroad	28%
Watching TV/soaps	27%
Getting rowdy at a football match	23%
Not being able to complain	15%
Loving karaoke	6%
Being unattractive	4%

67% of adults in the UK describe themselves as British, but **33%** of UK adults don't feel an association with being British

61% of **English** people would describe themselves as English rather than British, **83%** of **Scots** identify themselves as more Scottish than British and **70%** of **Welsh** feel more Welsh than British.

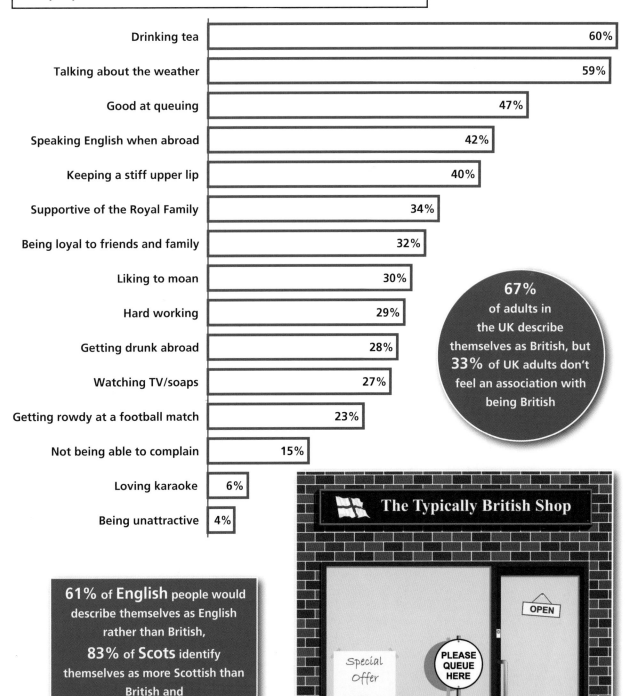

The Typically British Shop

Special Offer
TEA
buy 1 get 1 free

PLEASE QUEUE HERE

OPEN

Base: 2,012 UK adults aged 18+ were surveyed in April 2011

SEE ALSO:
Born and bred a Brit – but apparently I know nothing about Britishness. p24, Essential Articles 13
www.completeissues.co.uk

Source: Opinium Research 2011
www.opinium.co.uk

Community spirit

86% of people think their local area is a place where people from different backgrounds get along well

Where do communities mix?

% who have mixed socially with people from different ethnic or religious backgrounds in the last month, 2010-11, England

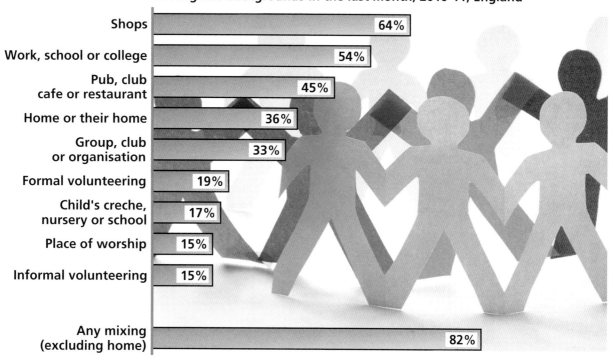

- Shops — **64%**
- Work, school or college — **54%**
- Pub, club cafe or restaurant — **45%**
- Home or their home — **36%**
- Group, club or organisation — **33%**
- Formal volunteering — **19%**
- Child's creche, nursery or school — **17%**
- Place of worship — **15%**
- Informal volunteering — **15%**
- Any mixing (excluding home) — **82%**

Who mixes most?

% mixing at least once a month with people from different ethnic or religious backgrounds, England

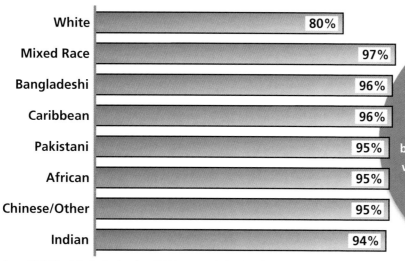

- White — **80%**
- Mixed Race — **97%**
- Bangladeshi — **96%**
- Caribbean — **96%**
- Pakistani — **95%**
- African — **95%**
- Chinese/Other — **95%**
- Indian — **94%**

People from ethnic minority groups were more likely than white people to mix socially with those from different ethnic or religious backgrounds – this could be due to where people live ie white people who lived in more ethnically diverse areas were likely to mix more with the different communities

Base: 10,000 adults in England and Wales, an ethnic minority boost sample of 5,000 and a Muslim boost sample of 1,200

Source: Citizenship survey 2010-2011
© Crown copyright 2011
www.communities.gov.uk

SEE ALSO:
www.completeissues.co.uk

Integrating immigrants

There are still many obstacles for immigrants to overcome in living, working or participating in our societies, but this is changing slowly

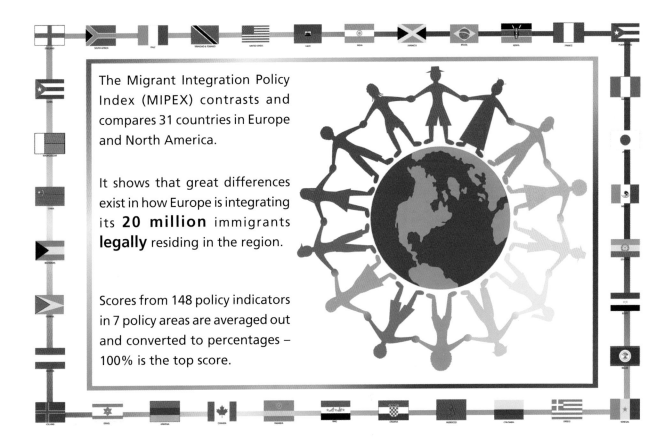

The Migrant Integration Policy Index (MIPEX) contrasts and compares 31 countries in Europe and North America.

It shows that great differences exist in how Europe is integrating its **20 million** immigrants **legally** residing in the region.

Scores from 148 policy indicators in 7 policy areas are averaged out and converted to percentages – 100% is the top score.

Overall, countries tend to score around **50%**. Most countries are creating as many **obstacles** as **opportunities** for immigrants to become equal members of society:

Opportunities

Migrant workers, **reunited families** and **long-term residents** enjoy basic security, rights and protection from **discrimination**.

Obstacles

The three greatest obstacles are for settled foreigners to become **citizens** or **politically active** and for all children, whatever their background, to learn and achieve together in **school**.

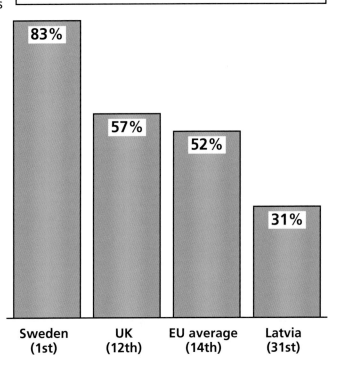

Top and bottom ranked countries overall, with UK and EU for comparison

83%	57%	52%	31%
Sweden (1st)	UK (12th)	EU average (14th)	Latvia (31st)

United Kingdom

overview compared to best and worst scoring countries in each policy area

Anti-discrimination

Whether religious/racial discrimination is punished and victims are encouraged to bring forward cases.

The UK has some of the strongest anti-discrimination laws and equality policies.

✔ Best: Canada 89%
✘ Worst: Latvia 25%

Political participation

Whether non-EU migrants can vote, stand as candidates in elections and are informed about political rights.

✔ Best: Norway 94%
✚ Worst: Romania 8%

Labour market

Whether immigrants are excluded from certain jobs and what rights they have as workers.

✚ Best: Sweden 100%
Worst: Cyprus & Slovakia 21%

Long-term residence

How long migrants have to wait to become long term residents.

✔ Best: Belgium 79%
✘ Worst: UK 31%

Access to nationality

How long they must wait to become citizens.

✔ Best: Portugal 82%
✘ Worst: Latvia 15%

Family reunion

Whether migrants can sponsor a relative and whether the state protects a migrant's right to settle with their family.

✔ Best: Portugal 91%
✘ Worst: Ireland 34%

Education

How well a migrant child progresses through the education system. Migrant pupils receive better support in British schools than on the continent, and all British pupils receive the best education on living in a diverse society.

✔ Best: Sweden 77%
✘ Worst: Hungary 12%

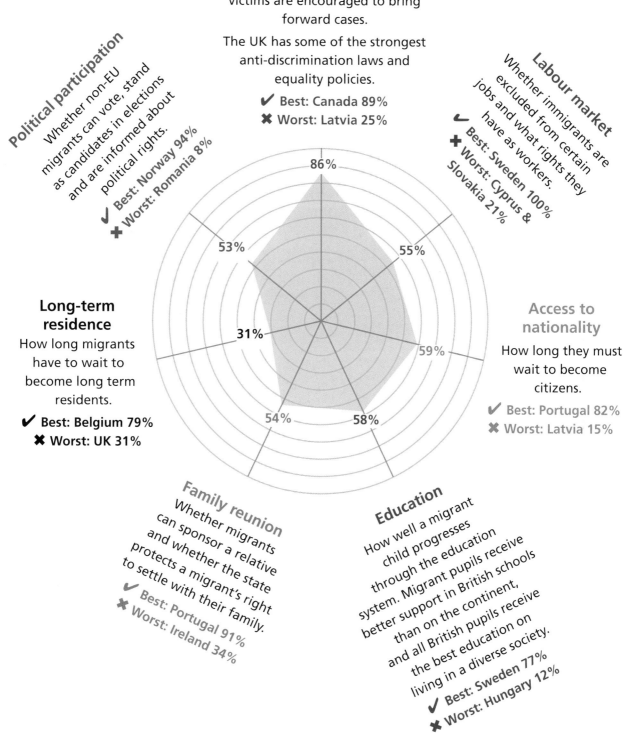

Radar chart values: 86%, 55%, 59%, 58%, 54%, 31%, 53%

SEE ALSO:
Who do you think you are? p26, Fact File 2011
Migrant workers, p29, Fact File 2011

www.completeissues.co.uk

Source: Migrant Integration Policy Index (MIPEX), British Council and the Migration Policy Group
www.mipex.eu

Equals

Most people believe that household tasks should be shared equally between men and women – but the reality is different

A survey of 1,028 adults aged 15+ looked at whether gender stereotypes are still present today in the workplace and the home. The survey results were released on the 100th anniversary of International Women's Day in 2011.

47% of women in the UK **do not** believe they are treated equally to men but **34%** believe they are.

Only around **35%** of men **do not** believe women are treated equally while **52%** believe they are.

60% of young women aged 15-30 had experienced sexist behaviour such as being whistled at, having sexist comments directed at them, or being discriminated against because of their gender.

In Britain today, who, if anyone, do you think currently **has more** responsibility and who do you think **should** have responsibility for the following?	Women		Men		Shared equally	
	Currently	Should have	Currently	Should have	Currently	Should have
Caring for their children	57%	17%	2%	2%	39%	81%
Earning money for their family	2%	1%	46%	25%	51%	72%
Managing household bills	31%	9%	16%	10%	50%	80%
Cooking meals for their family	57%	23%	4%	3%	38%	74%
Putting the bins out	14%	4%	44%	30%	40%	65%
Disciplining their children	28%	8%	10%	5%	59%	86%
DIY in the home	4%	1%	70%	49%	24%	49%
Keeping the home clean	64%	22%	2%	2%	33%	75%

The remaining % didn't know

Which, if any, of the following do you think would be the TWO key signs that men and women are truly equal in British society? When...

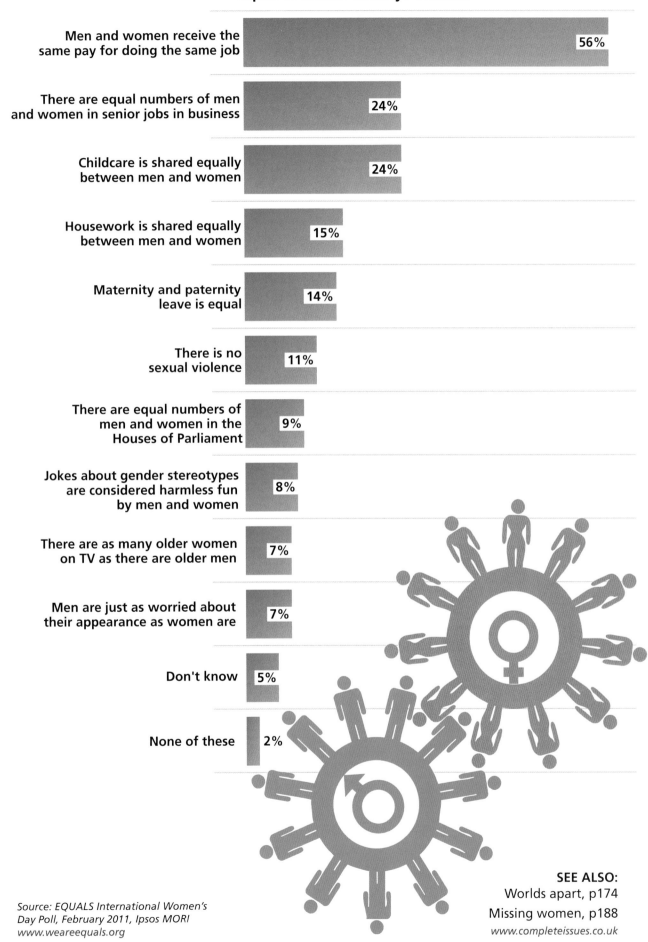

Men and women receive the same pay for doing the same job	56%
There are equal numbers of men and women in senior jobs in business	24%
Childcare is shared equally between men and women	24%
Housework is shared equally between men and women	15%
Maternity and paternity leave is equal	14%
There is no sexual violence	11%
There are equal numbers of men and women in the Houses of Parliament	9%
Jokes about gender stereotypes are considered harmless fun by men and women	8%
There are as many older women on TV as there are older men	7%
Men are just as worried about their appearance as women are	7%
Don't know	5%
None of these	2%

Source: EQUALS International Women's Day Poll, February 2011, Ipsos MORI
www.weareequals.org

SEE ALSO:
Worlds apart, p174
Missing women, p188
www.completeissues.co.uk

Generation Rent

From a nation of home owners we are becoming a nation of renters

What is Generation Rent?

64% of non homeowners can be defined as 'Generation Rent' – a generation with no realistic prospect of owning their own home in the next five years or who lack the long-term saving mentality that most need if they are to get on the housing ladder.

In short, they either cannot get on the property ladder (**40%** of non homeowners) or they do not wish to own their own home (**23%** of non homeowners).

Home ownership by age group

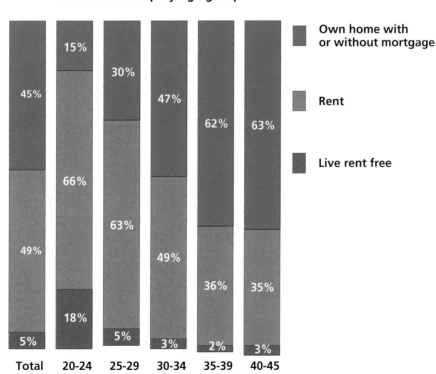

Legend:
- Own home with or without mortgage
- Rent
- Live rent free

Want to buy...

Wanting to own a home has been in Britain's DNA since the 1950s when living standards began to rise. The desire to own a home now is just as strong. **79%** of people see buying property as a good investment.

But only **5%** of Generation Rent are saving and making sacrifices to their lifestyle to get a deposit together, while **95%** say they have no spare cash to save, no interest in saving for a deposit or are trying to save but failing to do so.

What is stopping Generation Rent?

Most significant barriers preventing people who would like to buy their first home from doing so

Barrier	Percentage
The size of the deposit required	67%
High property prices	52%
Low income	41%
Lack of job security	31%
Higher mortgage repayments because of relatively small deposits	22%
Lenders' unrealistic expectations of people's credit histories	20%
Not feeling able to apply for a mortgage because they believe most applications are rejected	18%
Other debts	16%
Extra fees (eg solicitors'/ mortgage arrangement fees)	15%
Finding the right property	8%
Not knowing how to apply for a mortgage	6%
Stamp duty (tax applied to legal documents)	6%

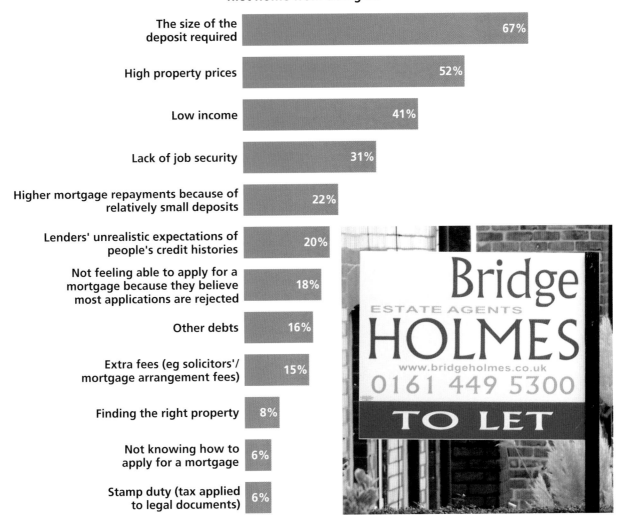

... but can't buy

Whilst finances are seen as the main barriers to home ownership, there is also fear of the mortgage process and of having a mortgage application declined.

This, combined with the difficulty of saving for a deposit, is driving a change in home ownership.
The majority of people think that banks do not want to lend to first time buyers (**84%**). Most people (**92%**) see it as hard for first time buyers to get a mortgage.

Base: 8,001 people aged 20-45 in an online survey

The Reality of Generation Rent – Perceptions of the First Time Buyer Market, Natcen
www.natcen.ac.uk

SEE ALSO:
Locked out, p112, Fact File 2011
Supply and demand, p110, Fact File 2011
Let's take the housing fight to wealthy owners with empty spare rooms, p50, Essential Articles 14
www.completeissues.co.uk

Who are you?

If you were leaving a time capsule for people in the future to learn about you and your life, what would you list as...

...the person who has been the greatest inspiration to you?
(top ten answers)

Parent	34%
Partner	7%
Grandparent	4%
Nelson Mandela	4%
Winston Churchill	3%
Son/daughter/children	2%
Margaret Thatcher	2%
Teacher	2%
Jesus Christ	2%
Diana, Princess of Wales	1%

...the object that best defines who you are?
(top ten answers)

PC/Computer/laptop	10%
House	5%
Car	4%
Mobile phone	4%
Books	3%
Family	2%
The Bible	2%
Wedding ring	2%
TV	1%
iPod/MP3 player	1%

...the word that best describes your outlook on life?
(top ten answers)

Optimistic	22%
Positive	9%
Hopeful	6%
Happy	4%
Pessimistic	3%
Realistic	2%
Relaxed	2%
Easy-going	1%
Laid-back	1%
Cautious	1%

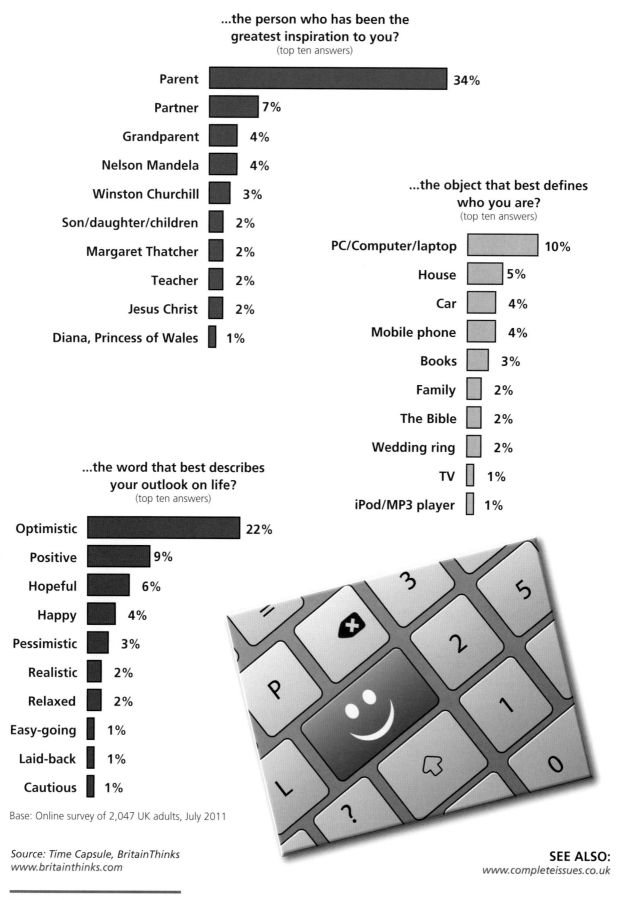

Base: Online survey of 2,047 UK adults, July 2011

Source: Time Capsule, BritainThinks
www.britainthinks.com

SEE ALSO:
www.completeissues.co.uk

Education

Only average

What is a typical secondary school?

Size of school, by pupil numbers

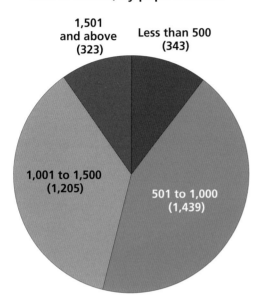

1,501 and above (323)

Less than 500 (343)

1,001 to 1,500 (1,205)

501 to 1,000 (1,439)

There are **3,310** secondary schools in England

Their sizes range from **5** with **100 pupils or fewer** to **221** with **more than 1,601 pupils**

The most common number of students for a school to have is between **801** and **900** – **11.2%** of schools

1,331 schools – **40.2%** — have pupil numbers between **701** and **1,100**

88% of secondary students are in schools with **more than 700 pupils**

89.7% of pupils are in classes of **30** pupils or less

10.3% of pupils are in classes of **31** pupils or more

In a class of 30 pupils:

There would be about **equal numbers** of **boys** and **girls**

Language:

26 would have English as their first language

For **3 or 4** it would not be their mother tongue

Ethnic background:

7 would come from a variety of ethnic backgrounds...

... the rest – **23** – would be white British

'Gifted and talented' and 'free school meals'

4 of the group would be classed as gifted and talented

5 would be claiming free school meals

Only **7.5%** of gifted and talented students claim free school meals

Travel to school:

13 walked to school, **10** came by bus, **6** by car, **1** (perhaps) came by bike – a very small number might have come by train or by some other means

NB figures may not add up due to rounding

Source: Schools, pupils and their characteristics, Department for Education © Crown copyright 2011 www.education.gov.uk

SEE ALSO:
Those who can... teach, p46, Fact File 2011
The class divide: how to teach boys and girls, p64, Essential Articles 14
'Super head' makes failing school most improved in England, p62, Essential Articles 13
www.completeissues.co.uk

Teacher talk

Many teachers say they love their job but ...

...they don't get the respect and support they need:

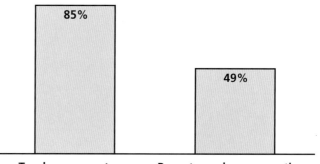

85%	49%
Teachers are not as respected in the UK as they are in other countries	Parents are less supportive than when they started out as teachers

...pupils are naughtier now than when they started teaching:

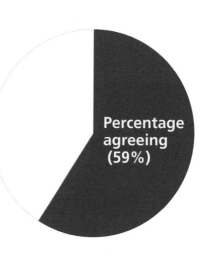

Percentage agreeing (59%)

Teachers think the reasons for this are:

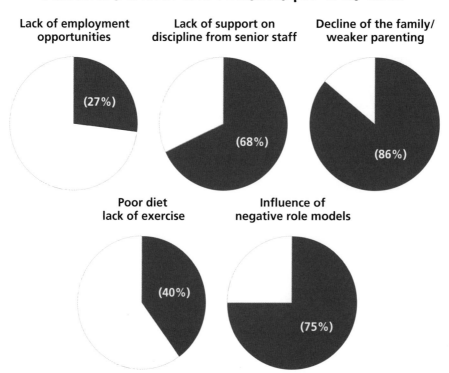

Lack of employment opportunities (27%)

Lack of support on discipline from senior staff (68%)

Decline of the family/ weaker parenting (86%)

Poor diet lack of exercise (40%)

Influence of negative role models (75%)

What do teachers think of their career prospects?

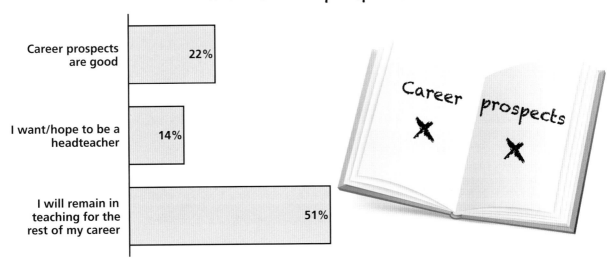

Career prospects are good	22%
I want/hope to be a headteacher	14%
I will remain in teaching for the rest of my career	51%

In its online survey of teacher opinion the Guardian newspaper received 2,000 completed replies from teachers. Many comments began: "I love teaching but ..."
or
"This is the best job in the world but ..."

SEE ALSO:
The issue: uniform... p60, Essential Articles 14

Name calling... if only I could, p204, Essential Articles 14

www.completeissues.co.uk

Source: The Guardian Teacher Network Poll, August 2011
www.guardian.co.uk/teacher-network/teacher-blog/2011/oct/03/i-love-teaching-but

Classroom crackdown

Parents and students agree that there should be more discipline – but don't agree on the methods

91% of parents and 62% of students agree that teachers should be allowed to be **tougher** when it comes to discipline. Similarly 93% of parents and

68% students agree that teachers need to have **more authority**. However, when it comes to ways of achieving this, opinions begin to differ.

How strongly do you agree or disagree that each of the following things is an acceptable form of discipline by teachers?

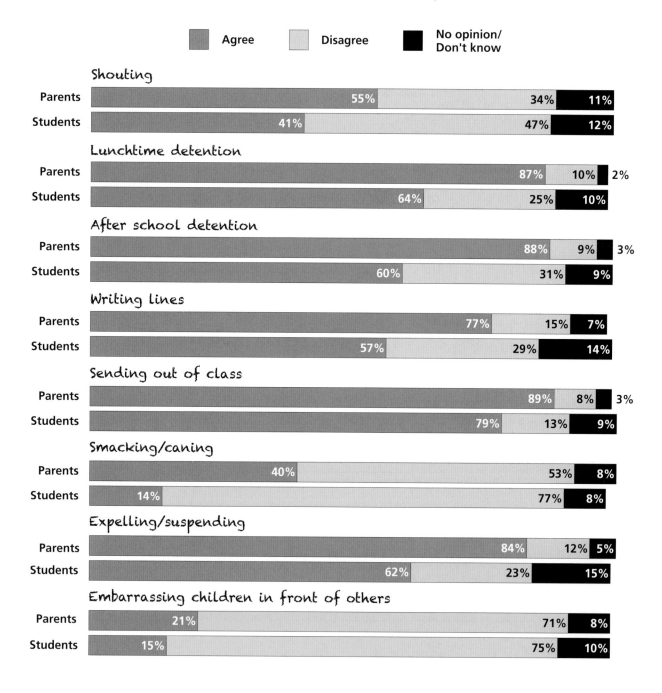

Agree   Disagree   No opinion/ Don't know

Shouting
Parents — 55% | 34% | 11%
Students — 41% | 47% | 12%

Lunchtime detention
Parents — 87% | 10% | 2%
Students — 64% | 25% | 10%

After school detention
Parents — 88% | 9% | 3%
Students — 60% | 31% | 9%

Writing lines
Parents — 77% | 15% | 7%
Students — 57% | 29% | 14%

Sending out of class
Parents — 89% | 8% | 3%
Students — 79% | 13% | 9%

Smacking/caning
Parents — 40% | 53% | 8%
Students — 14% | 77% | 8%

Expelling/suspending
Parents — 84% | 12% | 5%
Students — 62% | 23% | 15%

Embarrassing children in front of others
Parents — 21% | 71% | 8%
Students — 15% | 75% | 10%

Base: 2,014 UK parents with children in secondary school education, and 530 children currently studying at secondary schools

NB Figures may not add up to 100% due to rounding

Although parents and students are united in saying that teachers should not embarrass students, they disagree about the **qualities** they value in a teacher

Qualities (more than one quality could be chosen)	Parents	Students
Strictness	41%	26%
Ability to induce fear	8%	6%
Ability to command respect	81%	41%
A sense of authority	79%	37%
Relaxed approach/attitude	27%	57%
Patience	78%	68%
Calmness	65%	55%
Friendliness/matey with children	17%	58%
A sense of humour	65%	80%
Ability to inspire	86%	57%
Academic rigour	33%	15%
Passion for their subject	84%	59%
None of these	0%	1%
Don't know	1%	3%

Students seem to prioritise fun and interesting personality traits above respect and authority, which is preferred by their parents.

There was also a big difference in opinion as to who would make an **ideal teacher**

36% of **students** thought the Harry Potter character **Albus Dumbledore** would make an **ideal male teacher**, compared to **24%** of **parents**.

40% of **parents** chose **Stephen Fry** but only **17%** of **students** and **35% of parents** chose **David Attenborough** compared to **11%** of **students**

The divide continued with **ideal female teachers**. **48%** of **parents** but only **15%** of **students** thought **Carol Vorderman** would make an ideal teacher

40% of **students** would prefer **JK Rowling** compared to **31%** of **parents**

Source: Yougov survey, Aug-September 2011
http://today.yougov.co.uk

SEE ALSO:
The issue: uniform... p60, Essential Articles 14
My third-class life, p60, Essential Articles 13
www.completeissues.co.uk

Forced out?

Bullying is a problem for many children – and for some it means missing out on education

The Tellus4 online survey contains results from **253,755** children and young people in Years 6, 8 and 10 in **3,699** schools.

Bullying was an issue for **almost half** of them.

25% said they **often worried** about it – and **16%** of those said they **would not talk** to parents or carers about their concerns. **46%** said they had been bullied while **at school**

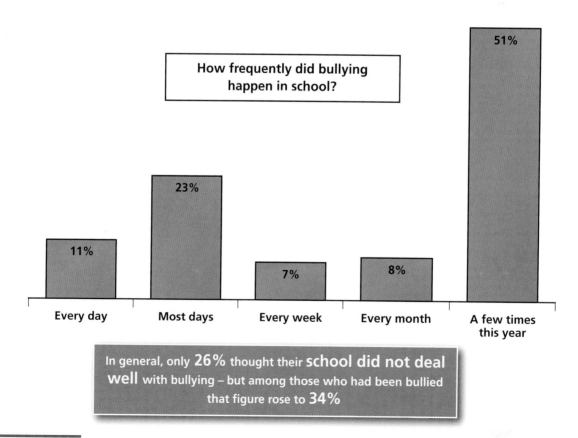

How frequently did bullying happen in school?

Every day	Most days	Every week	Every month	A few times this year
11%	23%	7%	8%	51%

In general, only **26%** thought their **school did not deal well** with bullying – but among those who had been bullied that figure rose to **34%**

For some young people the bullying is so severe that they skip school to avoid it. Red Balloon Learner Centres were set up specifically to help those children. This charity surveyed approximately 4,000 pupils who had 28 or more half sessions of absence.

From their results they estimated that about **13,985** students would give bullying as their main reason for absence from school and **71,980** young people would give this as one of their reasons for absence

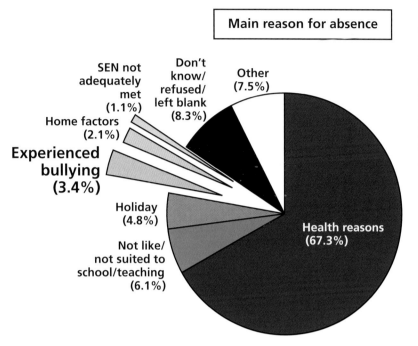

Main reason for absence

SEN not adequately met (1.1%)
Home factors (2.1%)
Experienced bullying (3.4%)
Don't know/ refused/ left blank (8.3%)
Other (7.5%)
Holiday (4.8%)
Not like/ not suited to school/teaching (6.1%)
Health reasons (67.3%)

People who gave 'bullying' and 'health' as the main reasons for absence also gave several other reasons, suggesting the complex nature of bullying. It seems likely that there is a close relationship between bullying and health problems – health problems could result from bullying or they could be a reason for a victim being targeted by bullies.

'Other' reasons include: misbehaviour, not suited to or not liking school, (pupils) peer pressure, moral or religious reasons, family caring responsibilities, cost or lack of equipment/uniform, unspecified.

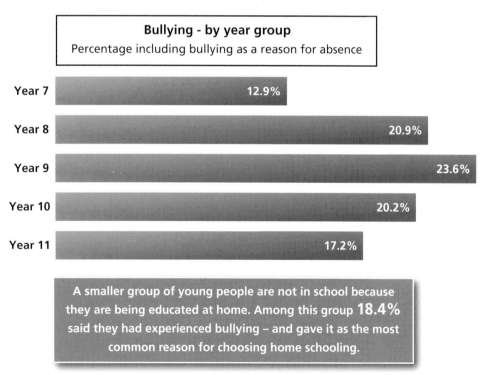

Bullying - by year group
Percentage including bullying as a reason for absence

Year 7   12.9%
Year 8   20.9%
Year 9   23.6%
Year 10   20.2%
Year 11   17.2%

A smaller group of young people are not in school because they are being educated at home. Among this group **18.4%** said they had experienced bullying – and gave it as the most common reason for choosing home schooling.

SEE ALSO:
www.completeissues.co.uk

Source: Tellus4 National Report 2010
© Crown copyright 2010
www.education.gov.uk
www.nfer.ac.uk

Source: Estimating the prevalence of young people absent from school due to bullying, May 2011
www.redballoonlearner.co.uk

True faith?

60% of people think group worship should not be enforced in schools

The Department for Education states that all maintained schools in England must provide a daily act of collective worship which must reflect the traditions of this country, which it says are, in the main, broadly Christian.

However, not everyone thinks this should be enforced. Some schools are opting to teach pupils about community rather than religion.

Do you think the requirement to provide a daily act of collective worship in schools **should** be enforced?
Percentage who said YES:

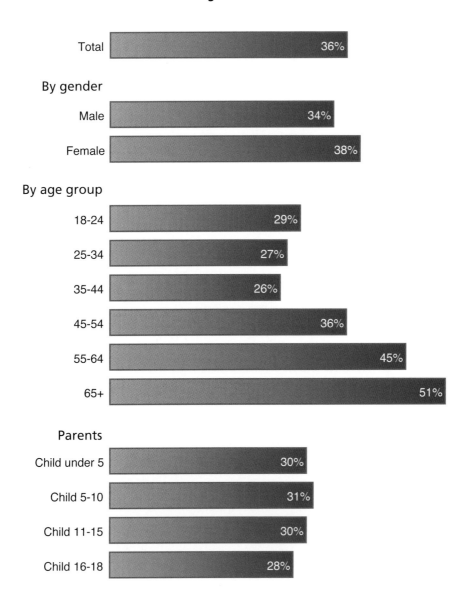

Total	36%
By gender	
Male	34%
Female	38%
By age group	
18-24	29%
25-34	27%
35-44	26%
45-54	36%
55-64	45%
65+	51%
Parents	
Child under 5	30%
Child 5-10	31%
Child 11-15	30%
Child 16-18	28%

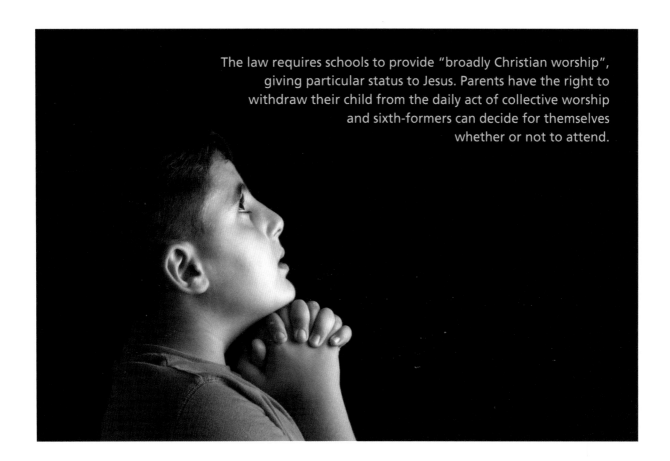

The law requires schools to provide "broadly Christian worship", giving particular status to Jesus. Parents have the right to withdraw their child from the daily act of collective worship and sixth-formers can decide for themselves whether or not to attend.

As far as you are aware, does your child attend collective group worship?

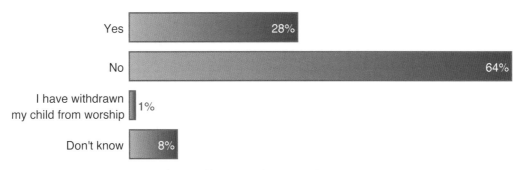

Yes 28%
No 64%
I have withdrawn my child from worship 1%
Don't know 8%

Figures do not add to 100% due to rounding

Difficult to do:

It appears that overall a majority of people are not in favour of enforcing collective group worship. Martin Cooper, deputy head teacher of Mile Oak School, near Brighton, said fulfilling the government's worship requirement was difficult. "In a school like ours, there isn't a great Christian ethos, so the message has to be a social one really."

Important to do:

Elaine Smith, head teacher at St Matthews Church of England Primary school in Blackburn, where 96% of the pupils are Muslims, said talking about faith regularly was beneficial. She said: "The majority of the pupils are children of faith and talk very openly about religion. The staff who are practising Christians or Muslims talk to the children and a bond is formed, which perhaps wouldn't be there if they didn't have the collective worship."

Source: BBC – Religion, worship in schools, ComRes
www.comres.co.uk
www.bbc.co.uk/news

SEE ALSO:
www.completeissues.co.uk

Reading progress

Many young people in the UK don't enjoy reading – how much does this matter?

The OECD ranked 65 countries in order based on how many 15 year olds said they **read for enjoyment**.

The UK ranked **47th** with **60.4%** of UK 15 year olds agreeing with this. This is slightly below the average of **62.6%** in developed (OECD) countries and well below the top country, **Kazakhstan**, at **92.8%**.

Time spent reading for enjoyment is strongly related to reading performance. Better readers tend to read more because they are more motivated to read, which, in turn, leads to improved vocabulary and comprehension skills.

But what about the 39.6% in the UK who don't ever enjoy reading? Does it matter?

Reading makes a difference

The OECD also runs PISA, the Programme for International Student Assessment.

In the latest survey, it tested **520,000** 15 year olds on a range of reading tasks. The assessment placed students at one of seven levels starting at a score of 262 – which 98.9% of students could reach – to scores above 698 which only the top 0.8% of students could reach.

The UK average of **494** was the **level reached by 57.2%** of students in the survey.

The average test score for all readers in **developed countries** was **493** points but for those who never read for enjoyment it was only **460** points.

What are they reading?

Percentage saying they read this material for enjoyment at least several times a month (OECD average)

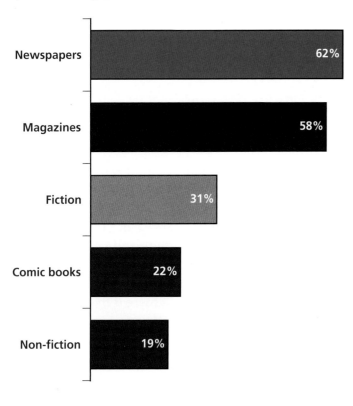

- Newspapers: 62%
- Magazines: 58%
- Fiction: 31%
- Comic books: 22%
- Non-fiction: 19%

What you read matters

Comparing reading test scores with what young people said about their reading habits showed that people who enjoyed reading became effective readers and the strongest readers were those who preferred to read fiction.

Average difference in reading scores between those who did read different materials and those who didn't

Those who read:
magazines
scored **15 more** points

newspapers
16 more points

Non-fiction
22 more points

Fiction
53 more points

Those who read **comic books** scored **3 points less** than the average. This could well be because weaker readers choose comic books as they are easier to read.

What's the picture in the UK?

Time spent reading for enjoyment – UK pupils

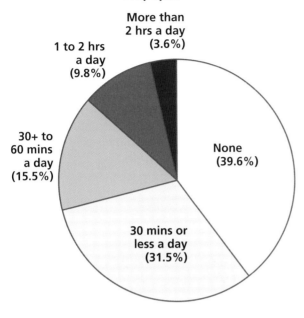

- More than 2 hrs a day (3.6%)
- 1 to 2 hrs a day (9.8%)
- 30+ to 60 mins a day (15.5%)
- 30 mins or less a day (31.5%)
- None (39.6%)

What difference does reading for enjoyment make?

The UK average score on the PISA tests is **494**

Students who don't read average **458** while those who do read score **521**

Scores and time spent reading

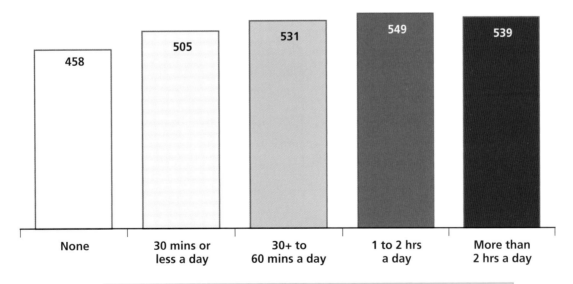

None	30 mins or less a day	30+ to 60 mins a day	1 to 2 hrs a day	More than 2 hrs a day
458	505	531	549	539

On average, students who read daily for enjoyment score the equivalent of one-and-a-half years of schooling better than those who do not.

Of those who read, the biggest difference in the UK scores is between those who **do not** read any fiction at **475** and those who do at **542.**

Source: PISA In Focus, Education at a Glance © OECD 2011
www.oecd.org

SEE ALSO:
www.completeissues.co.uk

Debt sentence

The recession has increased the strain of university costs and parents are finding it harder to support their child financially

49% of students now expect to graduate with **over £20,000** of debt and

13% think they will accumulate **over £30,000** of debt

Parents are, for the first time, in agreement with their children about the financial costs of university

50% of **parents** thought their child would graduate with **over £20,000** of debt

With the introduction of up to **£9,000** tuition fees in 2012:

21%

of tomorrow's students plan to choose a lower-charging university and

23%

of **parents** intend to encourage their children to choose a lower-charging university

As university costs mount up, those planning to go to university are thinking about living with parents during term-time to avoid debt:

38% of **parents** said it was **very** or **fairly likely** that their child will live at home during term time.

8% of students said they were planning to live with parents in term time to save money/ avoid debt and would do this happily.

Another **9%** said they were also planning to live with parents but would prefer not to.

3% said they would live with parents during term time but not for the full duration of the course.

Base: 1,522 parents of 13-18 year olds who have/ expect to have kids at university and 1,122 students

65% of **parents** contribute or plan to contribute financially to help their child through university:

24% of those parents will use **all or most** of their cash savings and

49% will use **some** of their cash savings.

A further **11%** plan to sell their financial investments

9% intend to sell their shares.

However, drastic measures are being taken by some **parents**:

6% planning to take out a bank loan,

6% planning to remortgage their house and

5% intending to downsize their house.

24% of **parents** were willing to sacrifice their annual holiday and

17% were willing to give up a new car and

13% willing to sacrifice home improvements to help their child through university.

61% of **students** are worried about job opportunities when they graduate in the light of the current state of the UK economy.

18% of **parents** think that a degree is not as valuable as it used to be

and a further **8%** are encouraging their child to seek vocational training rather than pursuing a degree.

25% of tomorrow's **students** would like to delay starting university for a year and work full time instead in order to save money.

32% of **students** who expect to be in debt were planning to look for better paid jobs in order to pay off their debt.

Source: Annual survey into student debt – YouGov survey for The Association of Investment Companies (AIC), 2011
www.theaic.co.uk

SEE ALSO:
Unifund, p43, Fact File 2010
www.completeissues.co.uk

Degree of debt

UK students entering higher education in 2011/12 should expect to owe around £26,100 on graduation

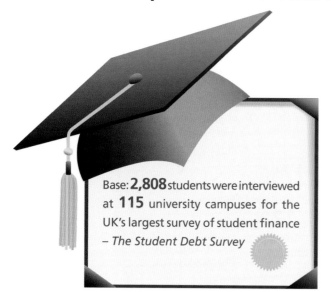

Base: **2,808** students were interviewed at **115** university campuses for the UK's largest survey of student finance – *The Student Debt Survey*

A student loan is meant to cover tuition fees and help with living costs such as housing, food, books, travel.

If you started university in 2012, you would begin to repay the loan (plus interest) when you had left university and you were earning above **£21,000 per year**.

The PUSH student debt survey showed that students starting university in **2011** could expect to graduate with total debts of **£26,100**. From **2012**, when tuition fees could be up to £9,000 a year, the average debt on graduation could be **£53,400**.

Average student debt per year, by country, 2011 UK

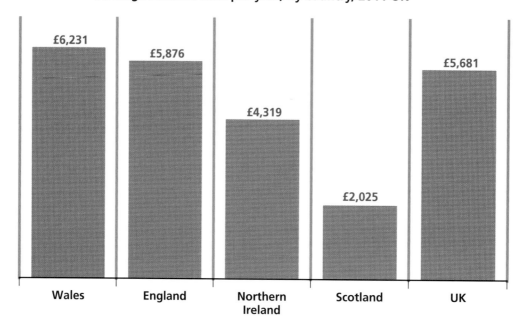

Wales	England	Northern Ireland	Scotland	UK
£6,231	£5,876	£4,319	£2,025	£5,681

The level of debt is lowest in Scotland where there is more support given to students and highest in Wales where there are fewer opportunities to earn money in part time jobs.

In October 2011, university applications for 2012 were running at **9%** below the previous year. Although the figures could change nearer to the deadline this may be a response to the rise in fees. In addition, a survey commissioned by the BBC suggested that higher fees would put off **10%** of potential students in England. Although most would probably still go to university, about half said they would consider a university closer to home to cut living costs, or one abroad with cheaper fees

Source: Student Debt Survey 2011, UCAS, BBC
www.push.co.uk
www.ucas.com
www.bbc.co.uk

SEE ALSO:
Unifund, p43, Fact File 2010
www.completeissues.co.uk

Environmental issues

Good behaviour

Shoppers are making more 'green' choices than a decade ago

How spending reflects ethical choices:

Food and drink

£6.5 billion was spent on products such as Fairtrade, Freedom foods, free range eggs and poultry etc – an increase of **27%** since 2007

Green home

£7.1 billion was spent on green energy, green mortgage repayments, energy efficient boilers etc – an increase of **8%** since 2007

Eco-travel and transport

£2.7 billion was spent on green cars, bicycles, public transport etc – an increase of **23%** since 2007

Personal products

£1.8 billion was spent on ethical clothing, cosmetics, charity shops etc – an increase of **29%** since 2007

Community

£5.8 billion was spent on local shopping, charitable donations etc – an increase of **6%** since 2007

Finance

£19.3 billion was spent on ethical banking and investments etc – an increase of **23%** since 2007

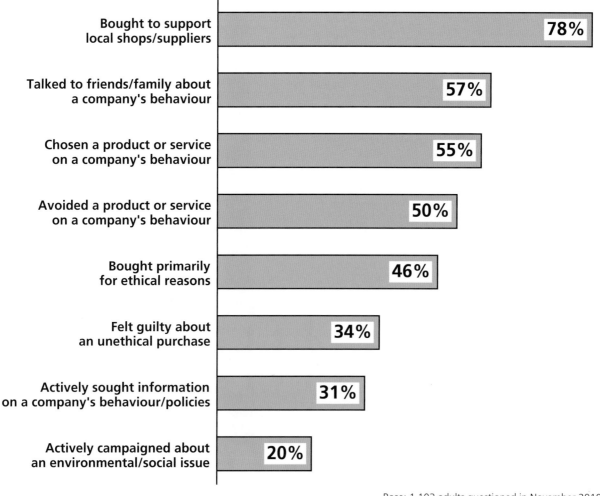

% of people saying they had done the following at least once during the year

Bought to support local shops/suppliers	78%
Talked to friends/family about a company's behaviour	57%
Chosen a product or service on a company's behaviour	55%
Avoided a product or service on a company's behaviour	50%
Bought primarily for ethical reasons	46%
Felt guilty about an unethical purchase	34%
Actively sought information on a company's behaviour/policies	31%
Actively campaigned about an environmental/social issue	20%

Base: 1,103 adults questioned in November 2010

£764
Average spend per household on ethical products and services

In 2009, the average spend per household on ethical products and services (excluding charitable donations and ethical finance) reached £764, 3 times that of 1999 when it was just £241.

From this amount, spending on green transport, energy efficiency and renewable energy has grown from just £23 in 1999 to reach £251 by 2009.

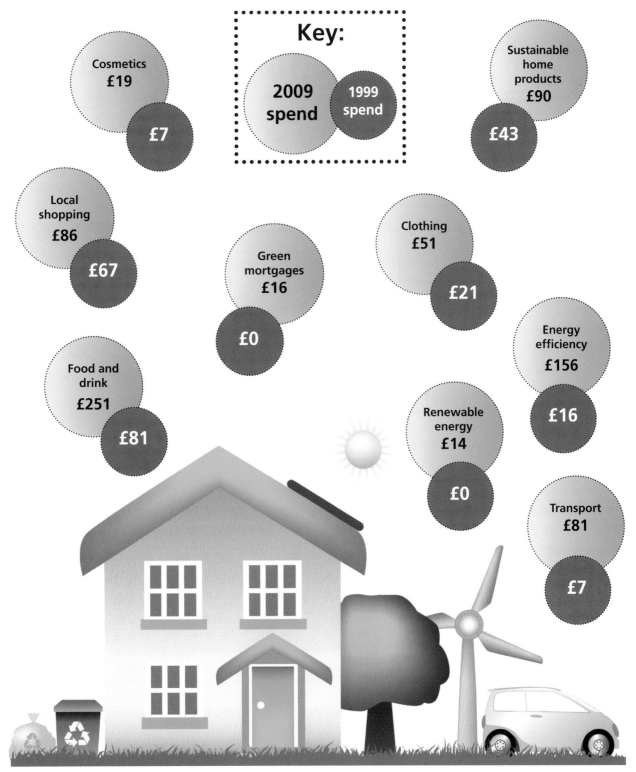

Key:

2009 spend | **1999 spend**

Cosmetics £19 — £7

Sustainable home products £90 — £43

Local shopping £86 — £67

Clothing £51 — £21

Green mortgages £16 — £0

Energy efficiency £156 — £16

Food and drink £251 — £81

Renewable energy £14 — £0

Transport £81 — £7

Source: Ethical Consumerism Report 2010
www.goodwithmoney.co.uk/ethicalconsumerismreport

SEE ALSO:
www.completeissues.co.uk

Stop the drop

Over 2.5 million pieces of litter are dropped on UK streets every day and almost half of us admit to dropping litter at some time

Litter is a major problem and has a big impact on the places where we live, work and play

Over

30 million tonnes

of litter are collected from England's streets every year and it costs council tax payers

£858 million a year

a year to clean it up

Keep Britain Tidy conducted a snapshot study in 30 key towns and cities across England on one day in January 2011, to assess which brands the public litter the most.

Types of litter

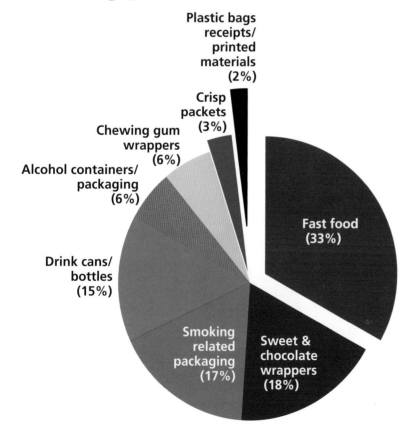

Plastic bags receipts/ printed materials (2%)

Crisp packets (3%)

Chewing gum wrappers (6%)

Alcohol containers/ packaging (6%)

Drink cans/ bottles (15%)

Fast food (33%)

Smoking related packaging (17%)

Sweet & chocolate wrappers (18%)

Fast food related litter was the most common.

Confectionery related litter is now the second most commonly found item, and has increased by **4%** since the previous study.

Smoking related litter has increased by **3%**.

Cigarette packaging makes up more than **50%** of the litter in the streets of the London area. In the 'City' area of London – which is the financial centre – the figure has risen from **14%** to **62%**

Most littered brands

The total amount of litter recorded
was made up of **224 brands**.

The **top 10 brands** littered were:

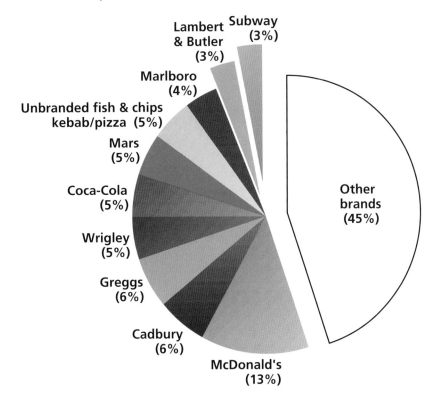

Subway
(3%)

Lambert
& Butler
(3%)

Marlboro
(4%)

Unbranded fish & chips
kebab/pizza (5%)

Mars
(5%)

Coca-Cola
(5%)

Wrigley
(5%)

Greggs
(6%)

Cadbury
(6%)

McDonald's
(13%)

Other
brands
(45%)

The **next 10 highest** are:

Nestlé 3%

Mayfair 2%

Walkers 2%

Lucozade and Ribena 2%

Benson & Hedges 2%

Richmond 1%

KFC 1%

Silk Cut 1%

Burger King 1%

Costa Coffee 1%

Results have been rounded to the closest
figure – where one or more brands show
the same result, the brands have been
ranked due to marginal difference

Keep Britain Tidy's
Love Where You Live
campaign is working with
some of the big companies –
McDonalds, Greggs, Wrigley
and Imperial Tobacco, whose
products end up as litter –
to try to tackle the problem
and educate customers to
take responsibility
for their litter

Source: Branded Litter Study 2010/11, Copyright © 2011 Keep Britain Tidy
www.keepbritaintidy.org

SEE ALSO:
www.completeissues.co.uk

Beachwatch

Beach litter has almost doubled over the last 15 years

The Marine Conservation Society organises the
Beachwatch Big Weekend every year.

4,927 volunteers helped to clean up and survey beaches
around the UK in September 2010.

376
beaches
were cleaned
amounting to
167 km around the UK

330,107
items of litter
were collected

3,058
bin bags
were filled

1,969
pieces of litter
were found for every
kilometre surveyed –
an increase of **6%**
from 2009

What was found?

(Number of items found, per km)

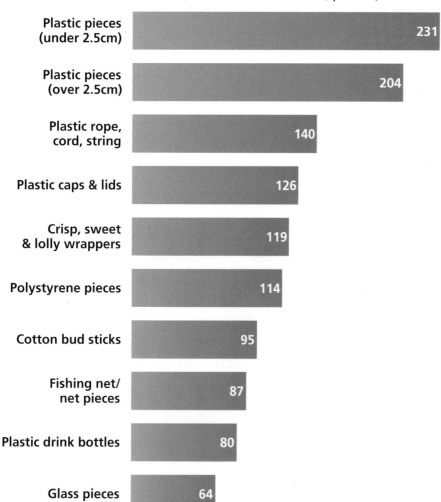

Plastic pieces (under 2.5cm)	231
Plastic pieces (over 2.5cm)	204
Plastic rope, cord, string	140
Plastic caps & lids	126
Crisp, sweet & lolly wrappers	119
Polystyrene pieces	114
Cotton bud sticks	95
Fishing net/ net pieces	87
Plastic drink bottles	80
Glass pieces	64

These **top ten** items
account for

64%

of all litter found

In total

72,943

plastic pieces
were found and removed

Since 1994, plastic items
found have **increased**
by **135%**

**Plastics may take
thousands of years
to fully break down
and sometimes never
leave the marine
environment**

Where does it all come from?

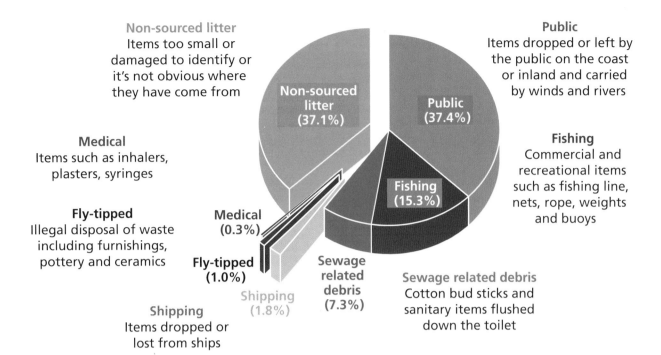

Non-sourced litter
Items too small or damaged to identify or it's not obvious where they have come from

Medical
Items such as inhalers, plasters, syringes

Fly-tipped
Illegal disposal of waste including furnishings, pottery and ceramics

Shipping
Items dropped or lost from ships

Public
Items dropped or left by the public on the coast or inland and carried by winds and rivers

Fishing
Commercial and recreational items such as fishing line, nets, rope, weights and buoys

Sewage related debris
Cotton bud sticks and sanitary items flushed down the toilet

Non-sourced litter (37.1%)
Public (37.4%)
Fishing (15.3%)
Medical (0.3%)
Fly-tipped (1.0%)
Shipping (1.8%)
Sewage related debris (7.3%)

What impact does it have?

- Marine litter can directly harm wildlife that eats it or gets tangled in it, causing death by starvation, drowning or suffocation.

- The fishing industry suffers lost earnings due to contamination of catches by litter and damage to fishing gear.

- Litter is unsightly and can have an effect on human health and local economies including a decline in tourism.

SEE ALSO:
The truth is hard to swallow, p68, Essential Articles 14
www.completeissues.co.uk

Source: Marine Conservation Society
www.mcsuk.org

Hidden waters

Fresh water is a scarce resource and demand is growing. We need to look at our personal 'water footprint'

In demand

In many parts of the world, the demand for water is already much greater than the available supply.

This affects developing countries, where many people do not have access to safe drinking water, and also the developed world, where our demand for water is becoming too high.

Under pressure

There are many reasons why the supply is under pressure: the world population explosion, rapid shifts of people from rural to urban areas, changes in eating habits as countries develop, pollution of water resources and too much groundwater being used up.

Climate change has an impact on our water resources too, making dry places even drier and wet ones too wet.

We use more water than we realise – in more ways

Each of us in the UK uses about **150 litres** of tap water a day. If you include the amount of water contained in products our water consumption is around **3,400 litres** every day.

How we use our **3,400 litres** a day

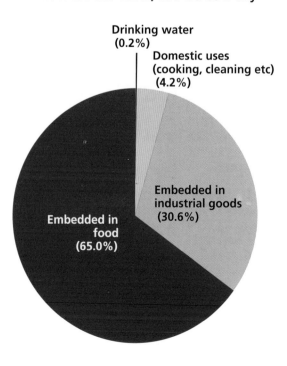

Drinking water
(0.2%)

Domestic uses
(cooking, cleaning etc)
(4.2%)

Embedded in
industrial goods
(30.6%)

Embedded in
food
(65.0%)

Food and non-food products like beer, burgers, clothing, cars and homes and even electricity all have water embedded in them.

We import many goods and services. Much of the embedded water that we consume, about **70%** of our **water footprint**, comes from other countries.

The **water footprint** is a way of measuring how much water we use as individuals and businesses.
It is measured in cubic metres per year –
1,000 litres = 1 cubic metre

65%

of the water we consume is in our food

Global average water footprint for selected items

2,400 litres

of water for one **burger**

Most of the water is needed for producing the beef contained in the burger

15,500 litres

of water per kg of **beef**

1,000 litres

of water for 1 litre of **milk**

Drinking a glass of milk (200ml) costs 200 litres of water – drinking the same volume of orange juice would cost 170 litres of water

Drinking a plain glass of water requires only little more than the water itself

5,000 litres

of water for 1kg of **cheese**

To produce 1kg of cheese we need 10 litres of milk

The volume of water required to produce this milk is 10,000 litres

The volume of water in 10 litres of milk gets divided equally into cheese and its by-product whey

30 litres

of water for one cup of **tea**

To produce 1kg of fresh tea leaves we require 2,400 litres of water

Altogether, the world population required about

30 billion cubic metres

of water per year in order to be able to drink tea

140 litres

for 1 cup of **coffee**

A standard 125ml cup of coffee needs more than 1,100 drops of water for producing one drop of coffee.

Drinking tea instead of coffee would save a lot of water

Source: Water Footprint Network; Waterwise
www.waterfootprint.org
www.waterwise.org.uk

SEE ALSO:
www.completeissues.co.uk

Nuclear future?

Nuclear power supplies around 14% of the world's electricity

- Nuclear generation began more than 50 years ago. Its main use is to generate electricity, using uranium as a fuel

- Uranium is a naturally occurring **radioactive** element, left over from the Earth's formation – it is not renewable

- The world's production of uranium comes mainly from **Kazakhstan – 33%, Canada – 18%** and **Australia – 11%**.

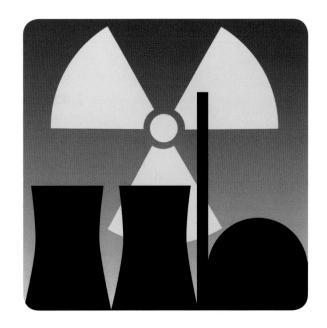

World nuclear power reactors & uranium requirements
Top ten countries, by number of nuclear reactors

Country	% of country's nuclear electricity generated 2009	Operating nuclear reactors April 2011	Uranium required 2011
	%	Number	Tonnes
USA	20.2	104	19,427
France	75.2	58	9,221
Japan	28.9	51	8,195
Russian Fed.	17.8	32	3,757
Korea (South)	34.8	21	3,586
India	2.2	20	1,053
UK	**17.9**	**19**	**2,235**
Canada	14.8	18	1,884
Germany	26.1	17	3,453
Ukraine	48.6	15	2,037

- Many countries have a strong commitment to nuclear power. Among these are China, India, the United States, Russia and Japan, which together make up half of the world population.

- More than **15 countries** rely on nuclear power for **25%** or more of their electricity.

- All but one of the **UK's 19** reactors will be retired by 2023. There are **4** new reactors on order or planned and **9** proposed.

Worldwide in April 2011 there were:

61
reactors being built

158
reactors on order or planned

326
proposed reactors

Nuclear outlook

Projections of worldwide growth of nuclear power based on the need,
the ability to generate, and the amount of commitment to nuclear power,
with population growth as a key factor

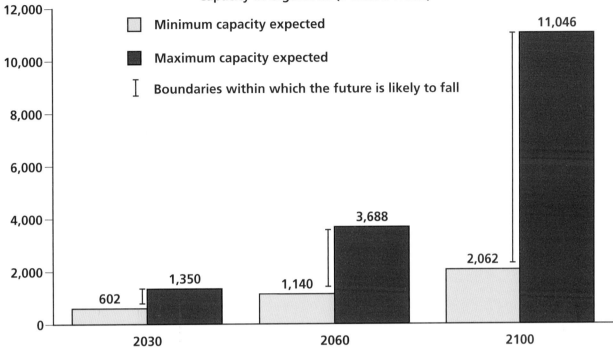

Capacity in Gigawatts (1 billion watts)

- ☐ Minimum capacity expected
- ■ Maximum capacity expected
- I Boundaries within which the future is likely to fall

2030: 602 / 1,350
2060: 1,140 / 3,688
2100: 2,062 / 11,046

**Nuclear power is the most controversial method of energy production
because of the material involved and long term consequences of accidents.**

For

*Some consider that nuclear power is a clean
energy source that reduces carbon emissions*

So it is our only hope of slowing global
warming and keeping our current lifestyle

Against

*Some believe that the toxic waste from the
power plants poses many threats to people
and the environment*

Storing the waste safely is extremely difficult –
particularly because it lasts for thousands
of years

On 11th March 2011 the Fukushima nuclear plant on the east coast of Japan was hit by a massive earthquake and tsunami, leading to some reactors overheating and leaking. A 20km exclusion zone was established and 80,000 people were evacuated.

In October 2011 it was reported that a complete clean up may take up to 30 years. Several countries suspended their reactor building programmes immediately after this disaster.

*Source: World Nuclear Association;
BBC Guide to Nuclear power*
www.world-nuclear.org
www.bbc.co.uk

SEE ALSO:
The nuclear debate, p66,
Essential Articles 14
www.completeissues.co.uk

Life on earth

We don't yet know the number of species on Earth – one of the most basic questions in science

The natural world contains about **8.7 million** species.

We have been identifying, grouping, and naming organisms for 250 years. Over **1.2 million** species are already entered in a central database, but some **86%** of the species on Earth, and **91%** of species in the ocean, have still not been given scientific descriptions.

Using the current rates of description from the last 20 years, the estimated time to classify the Earth's remaining species may be as long as **1,200 years.**

It would need **303,000** scientists and cost about **US$364 billion** to describe them all.

This slow progress will mean some species will become extinct before we know they even exist!

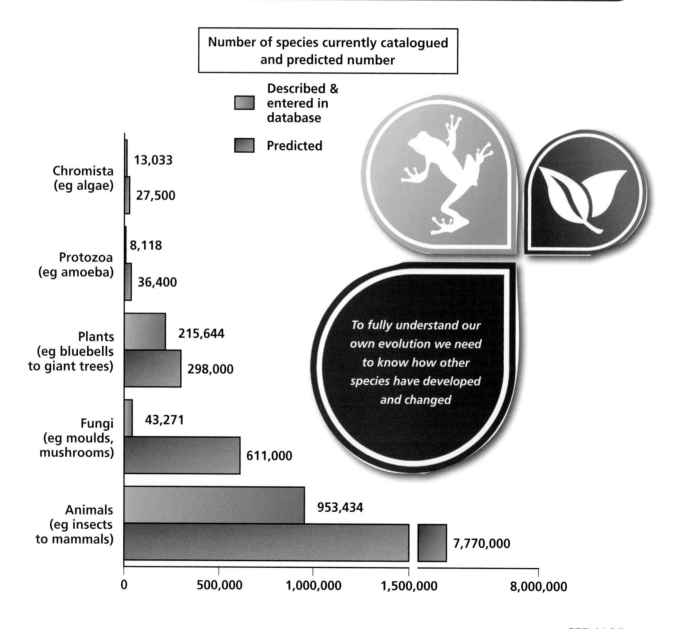

Number of species currently catalogued and predicted number

Described & entered in database

Predicted

	Described	Predicted
Chromista (eg algae)	13,033	27,500
Protozoa (eg amoeba)	8,118	36,400
Plants (eg bluebells to giant trees)	215,644	298,000
Fungi (eg moulds, mushrooms)	43,271	611,000
Animals (eg insects to mammals)	953,434	7,770,000

To fully understand our own evolution we need to know how other species have developed and changed

Source: Public Library of Science (PLoS Biology) August 2011
www.plosbiology.org

SEE ALSO:
Under threat, p17, Fact File 2010
Of all the species in all the world, which would we miss most? p11, Essential Articles 12
www.completeissues.co.uk

Family & relationships

Family friendly

The best places to bring up children

What makes a family friendly location?

Education

Quality of the local schools, school inspection results, Key Stage 2 results in English and Maths, truancy levels, amount and quality of early years provision and average child care costs

Safety

A safe environment for young ones to grow up in. Low frequency of burglary, robbery, vehicle crimes, anti-social behaviour and violent crime

Property

Levels of affordable housing, property prices compared to average local salaries, how quickly houses are selling and proportion of owner occupied property

Amenities

Services that support family life from toy shops and children's clothes stores to zoos, museums and cinemas with baby clubs. The best public parks and green spaces, closeness to leisure centres with children's swimming clubs and gym classes. Fast food restaurants and betting shops were given a negative score

Population

Sense of community where there are plenty of other children to play with. Age and birth rate of the population was taken into account to see how densely an area is populated with families with young children

When combined, the scores give a good measure of how desirable an area might be to young families.

The report looked at over 60 factors in five categories in almost 2,400 postcode districts across England and Wales. It aimed to find the best mix of family friendly factors eg high quality education and child care, low crime rates and access to amenities and affordable housing.

Points were given to each postcode district – any desirable factors were given a positive score while undesirable ones were given a negative score, eg a good nearby school would receive a positive score but a high number of burglaries in a residential area would receive a negative score.

Rural locations such as Winkleigh in Devon, the number one family friendly hotspot, feature highly because of their open green spaces and very low crime levels.

Sutton Coldfield, near Birmingham, which ranked 8th and Galgate near Lancaster, which ranked 3rd, are close to city centres and good urban parks and have top education attainment at Key Stage 2.

National top 10 places to bring up children and a selection from the 60 indicators

Place & postcode district	Average Key Stage 2 scores in Maths English	% Early Years care ranked outstanding	Crime per capita	Average price for 2 bed property	Average Salary	Overall Hotspot Score out of 25
National Average	27.47	12.2	0.05	£167,659	£24,170	
Winkleigh, Devon – EX19	29.15	16.7	0.01	£150,837	£37,566	19.76
South Petherton, Somerset – TA13	30.0	25.0	0.02	£158,823	£25,489	18.89
Galgate, Lancashire – LA2	30.5	20.7	0.02	£159,398	£25,749	18.86
Eaglescliffe, Stockton on Tees – TS16	29.62	9.1	0.03	£131,478	£26,459	18.83
Bromley Cross, Bolton – BL7	28.87	18.8	0.02	£140,046	£31,918	18.75
Shebbear, Devon – EX21	28.2	20.0	0.01	£173,254	£53,084	18.65
Great Ayton, North Yorks – TS9	29.97	22.0	0.03	£168,789	£30,270	18.60
Sutton Coldfield, West Midlands – B74	29.64	16.7	0.02	£171,464	£31,715	18.56
Moor Row, Cumbria – CA24	28.4	0	0.03	£76,548	£19,258	18.55
Bromyard, Herefordshire – HR7	29.6	60.0	0.03	£142,102	£37,857	18.53

The first **London** location, Sutton, is ranked at
20th, mainly due to the high cost of the property

Source: Family Investments – Family Friendly Hotspots Report 2011
www.family.co.uk/hotspots

SEE ALSO:
www.completeissues.co.uk

Safe house

No child should have to live in fear or on edge in their own home – that's the place they should feel safest

Pete, research participant

The NSPCC interviewed 2,275 children aged 11-17 years old about their experiences to give an up to date picture of childhood maltreatment in the UK

Around one in five children – **18.6%** – had been physically attacked by an adult, sexually abused, or severely neglected at home. This is equivalent to **973,000** secondary school children in the UK population.

6.9% had been physically attacked by an adult during childhood.

Parents or guardians were responsible for **55%** of the violent acts carried out against children.

4.8% had been sexually assaulted either by an adult or another child or young person.

3% had been raped or forced into sex by another child and **2%** had been sexually abused by an adult.

13.4% reported severe maltreatment by a parent or guardian at some point during childhood.

7.8% reported severe maltreatment by another adult during childhood.

3.3% reported serious physical violence by another adult and **1%** had been sexually assaulted by an adult.

Sexual abuse became more common during teenage years up to the age of 17. Girls were the main victims.

Photo posed by model

Severe emotional neglect or lack of physical care or supervision that would place a child at risk was the most common child maltreatment – suffered by **9.8%** of children.

Physical neglect – not getting enough food, not being taken to the doctor when ill and not having a safe place to stay – was experienced by **1.4%**.

With around **46,000** children of all ages currently on a child protection plan or register, the study by the NSPCC raises concern that the vast majority of abused and neglected children are not getting the vital help and support they need

Number of children on child protection registers or subject to a child protection plan

	2006	2007	2008	2009	2010
England	26,400	27,900	29,200	34,100	39,100
Scotland	2,288	2,593	2,433	2,682	2,518
Wales	2,165	2,325	2,320	2,510	2,730
Northern Ireland	1,639	1,805	2.071	2,488	2,361
UK	32,492	34,623	36,024	41,780	46,709

England and Scotland figures include unborn children
Wales data has been rounded to the nearest five

The study indicates that severely abused and neglected children are almost **nine times** more likely to kill themselves, and almost **five times** more likely to self-harm than children who have not been severely abused or neglected.

"Children need to know they've got support otherwise how are they going to be brave enough to say anything?"

Bella, research participant

ChildLine 0800 1111
NSPCC Helpline 0808 800 5000
Source: NSPCC - Child Cruelty in the UK 2011
www.nspcc.org.uk

SEE ALSO:
I sent my abusive father to jail – this is my story, p84, Essential Articles 14
www.completeissues.co.uk

Fact File 2012 • www.carelpress.com
Family & relationships 57

Could you tell?

As more children are subject to sexual exploitation, could you tell the signs?

Barnardo's, a charity that focuses on helping vulnerable children, works with many young people who have been 'groomed' by an abusing adult – often posing as a 'boyfriend figure'.

They say children are often befriended, lavished with gifts and attention and then gradually drawn into the control of the 'boyfriend' – essentially brainwashed so they are vulnerable to sexual exploitation.

Children and young people from any ethnic background are at risk, boys as well as girls.

Barnardo's asked parents if they believed that there were children who were being sexually exploited in the local area, or not?

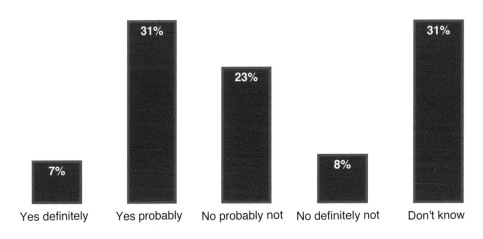

7%	31%	23%	8%	31%
Yes definitely	Yes probably	No probably not	No definitely not	Don't know

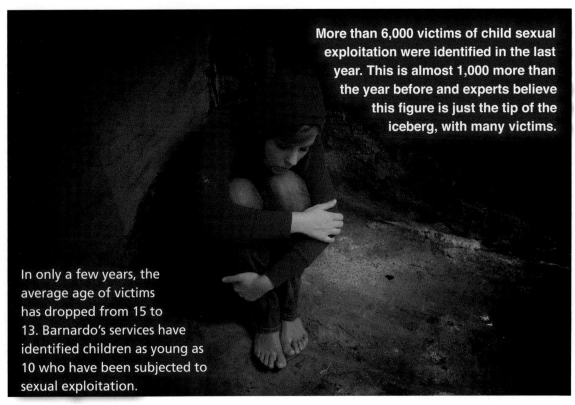

More than 6,000 victims of child sexual exploitation were identified in the last year. This is almost 1,000 more than the year before and experts believe this figure is just the tip of the iceberg, with many victims.

In only a few years, the average age of victims has dropped from 15 to 13. Barnardo's services have identified children as young as 10 who have been subjected to sexual exploitation.

Barnardo's asked parents which of these would you consider signs that a child may be being sexually exploited?

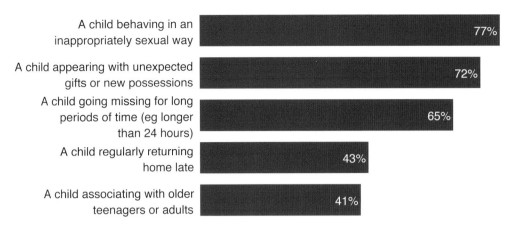

A child behaving in an inappropriately sexual way	77%
A child appearing with unexpected gifts or new possessions	72%
A child going missing for long periods of time (eg longer than 24 hours)	65%
A child regularly returning home late	43%
A child associating with older teenagers or adults	41%

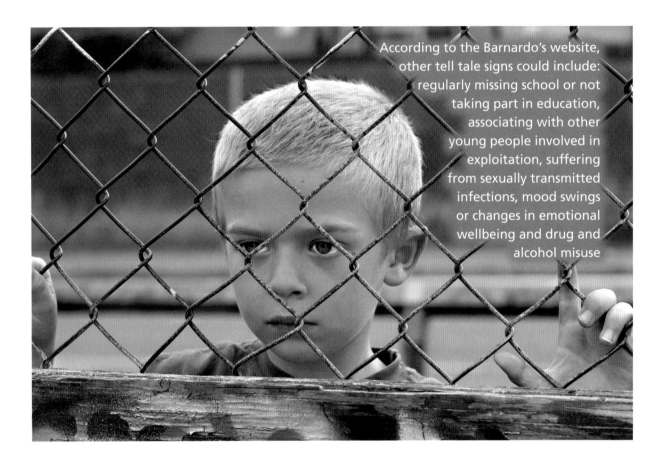

According to the Barnardo's website, other tell tale signs could include: regularly missing school or not taking part in education, associating with other young people involved in exploitation, suffering from sexually transmitted infections, mood swings or changes in emotional wellbeing and drug and alcohol misuse

Anne Marie Carrie, Barnardo's chief executive. said: "This is a horrific and pernicious crime that everybody needs to be alive to." Worryingly however, only 18% of dads and 25% of mums say they are very confident that they would spot whether their child was at risk of sexual exploitation.

Base: 1,147 parents aged 18-65+

Source: Barnardo's Public Poll August 2011, ComRes
www.barnardos.org.uk
www.comres.co.uk

SEE ALSO:
Fear of racism should no longer be the veil covering up hard truths, p110, Essential Articles 14
Too many of us treat young white women as trash, p112, Essential Articles 14
www.completeissues.co.uk

Someone to talk to

Most children and young people have some aspect of their lives they worry about ...

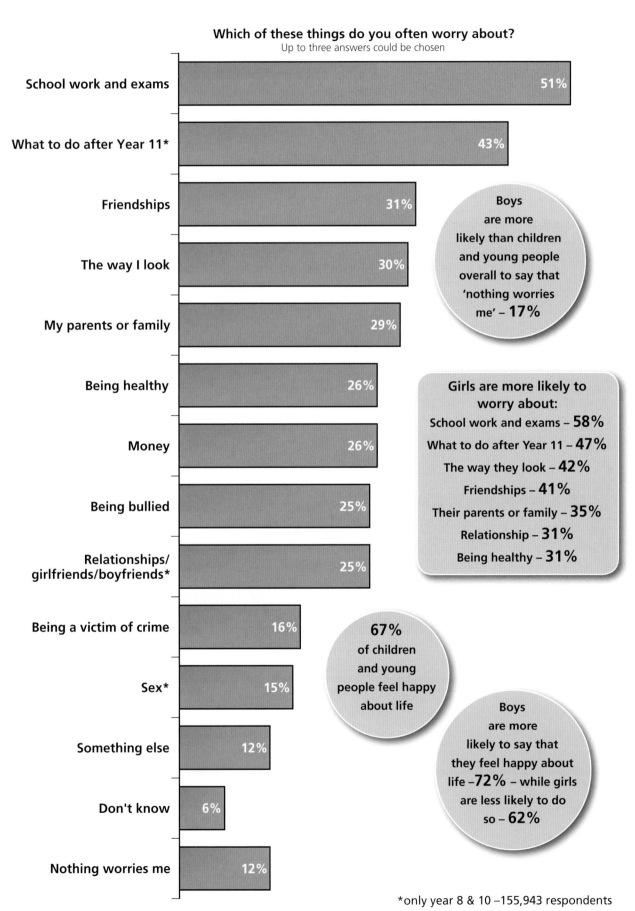

Which of these things do you often worry about?
Up to three answers could be chosen

Category	Percentage
School work and exams	51%
What to do after Year 11*	43%
Friendships	31%
The way I look	30%
My parents or family	29%
Being healthy	26%
Money	26%
Being bullied	25%
Relationships/girlfriends/boyfriends*	25%
Being a victim of crime	16%
Sex*	15%
Something else	12%
Don't know	6%
Nothing worries me	12%

Boys are more likely than children and young people overall to say that 'nothing worries me' – **17%**

Girls are more likely to worry about:
School work and exams – **58%**
What to do after Year 11 – **47%**
The way they look – **42%**
Friendships – **41%**
Their parents or family – **35%**
Relationship – **31%**
Being healthy – **31%**

67% of children and young people feel happy about life

Boys are more likely to say that they feel happy about life –**72%** – while girls are less likely to do so – **62%**

*only year 8 & 10 –155,943 respondents

Fact File 2012 • www.carelpress.com

... but most have relationships in their lives which support them

Percentage of children and young people saying:

When I'm worried about something...

...I can talk to my friends	66%
...I can talk to my mum or dad	64%
...I can talk to an adult who isn't my mum or dad	40%

Overall **85%** of children and young people say that they have **at least one person** that they can talk to. Only **3%** say they **can't talk to anyone** when worried.

About **20%** of children and young people feel they **can't discuss their worries** with their parent or carer or **don't know whether they could.**

However, this doesn't mean they have no-one to talk to as most of these – **60%** – say that they can talk to their **friends or another adult** when worried.

Nearly all children and young people – **92%** – have **one or more good friends.**

72% of girls and **59%** of boys say they talk to **their friends** when they are worried.

Base: 253,755 children and young people in Years 6, 8 and 10 in 3,699 primary, secondary and special schools and Pupil Referral Units

Source: Tellus4 National Report 2010, The Department for Education © Crown copyright 2010
www.education.gov.uk
www.nfer.ac.uk

SEE ALSO:
www.completeissues.co.uk

Under pressure

What parents think about the issues children might face today

From what you have seen, read, heard about or experienced, to what extent do you agree or disagree with the following statements about children in the UK today?

Legend: Agree | Neither agree/nor disagree | Disagree | Don't know

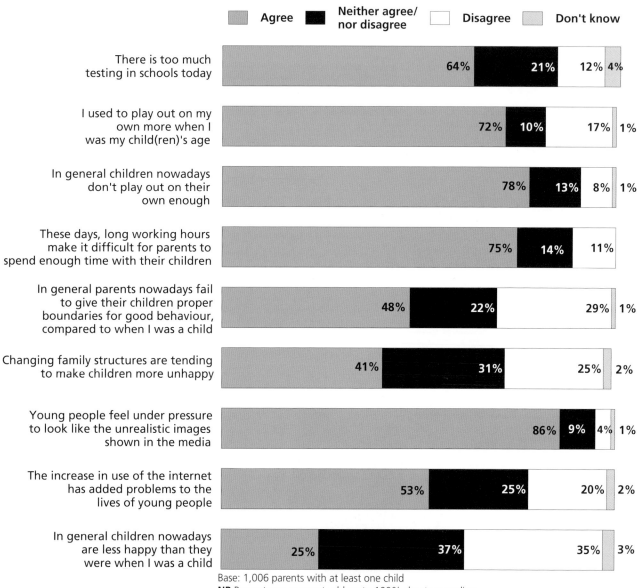

There is too much testing in schools today
64% | 21% | 12% | 4%

I used to play out on my own more when I was my child(ren)'s age
72% | 10% | 17% | 1%

In general children nowadays don't play out on their own enough
78% | 13% | 8% | 1%

These days, long working hours make it difficult for parents to spend enough time with their children
75% | 14% | 11%

In general parents nowadays fail to give their children proper boundaries for good behaviour, compared to when I was a child
48% | 22% | 29% | 1%

Changing family structures are tending to make children more unhappy
41% | 31% | 25% | 2%

Young people feel under pressure to look like the unrealistic images shown in the media
86% | 9% | 4% | 1%

The increase in use of the internet has added problems to the lives of young people
53% | 25% | 20% | 2%

In general children nowadays are less happy than they were when I was a child
25% | 37% | 35% | 3%

Base: 1,006 parents with at least one child
NB Percentages may not add up to 100% due to rounding

Source: Mumsnet survey, 2011
www.mumsnet.com

SEE ALSO:
A life worth living? p34, Fact File 2010

Actually, the kids are alright, p206, Essential Articles 14

I'd hate to be a teenage girl today, p101, Essential Articles 13

Parents' perspective, pg74, Fact File 2011

www.completeissues.co.uk

Finding families

**Only 60 babies in care were adopted last year...
is the process too slow and too cautious?**

Number of adoptions by year and age group

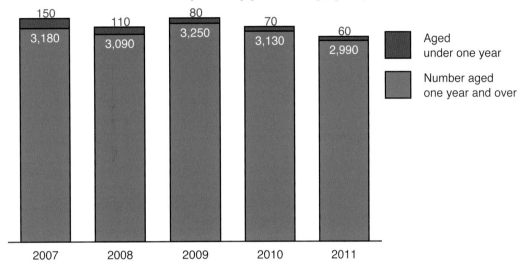

150	110	80	70	60
3,180	3,090	3,250	3,130	2,990
2007	2008	2009	2010	2011

Aged under one year

Number aged one year and over

Age at which children in care were adopted

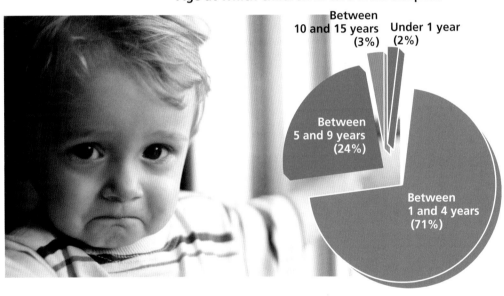

Between 10 and 15 years (3%)

Under 1 year (2%)

Between 5 and 9 years (24%)

Between 1 and 4 years (71%)

The average age of a child at the time of adoption was 3 yrs 10 months. There were a very small number of adoptions of children aged 16+

Between coming into care and the decision that the child should be adopted: **10 months**

Between that decision and matching the child with adopters: **8 months**

Between matching and placing for adoption: **1 month**

Between placing for adoption and the date the child is adopted: **9 months**

A child aged under one year will remain in care for two years and three months, on average, before being adopted

A spokesman for the charity Barnardo's said: "This is a tragedy for the children who are languishing in the care system and...for those people who have come forward and want to be parents and adopt a child"

Source: Office for National Statistics © Crown copyright 2011,
Department for Education, Adoption Register for England & Wales
www.ons.gov.uk
www.education.gov.uk
www.adoptionregister.org.uk

SEE ALSO:
Fostering prejudice, p82,
Essential Articles 14
www.completeissues.co.uk

Happy anniversary

The divorce rate has fallen to its lowest since 1974

The number of divorces in England and Wales in 2009 was **113,949**, a decrease of **6.4%** since 2008

The divorce rate fell in 2009 to **10.5** divorcing people per thousand married population from **11.2** in 2008

Men and women in their late twenties had the highest divorce rates of all age groups

In 2009 there were
21.7 males
divorcing per thousand married men in this age group and
25.1 females
divorcing per thousand married women

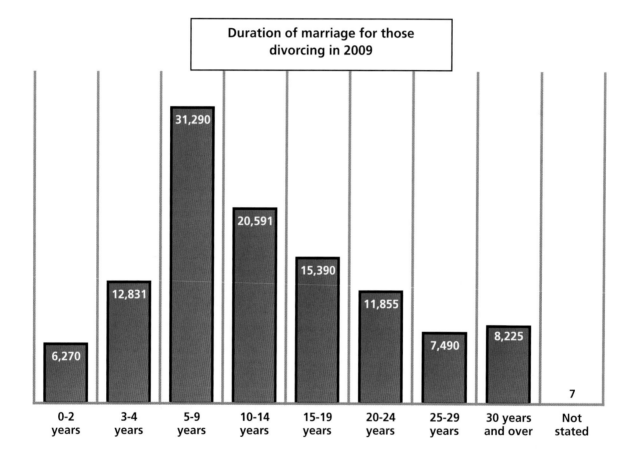

Duration of marriage for those divorcing in 2009

Duration	Number
0-2 years	6,270
3-4 years	12,831
5-9 years	31,290
10-14 years	20,591
15-19 years	15,390
20-24 years	11,855
25-29 years	7,490
30 years and over	8,225
Not stated	7

Cumulative percentage of marriages which ended in divorce

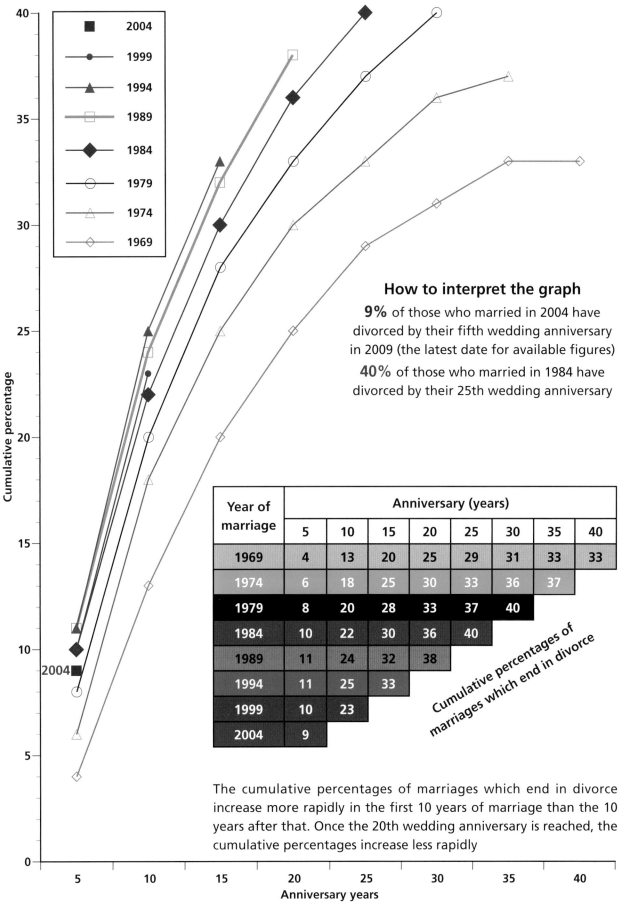

How to interpret the graph

9% of those who married in 2004 have divorced by their fifth wedding anniversary in 2009 (the latest date for available figures)

40% of those who married in 1984 have divorced by their 25th wedding anniversary

Year of marriage	Anniversary (years)							
	5	**10**	**15**	**20**	**25**	**30**	**35**	**40**
1969	4	13	20	25	29	31	33	33
1974	6	18	25	30	33	36	37	
1979	8	20	28	33	37	40		
1984	10	22	30	36	40			
1989	11	24	32	38				
1994	11	25	33					
1999	10	23						
2004	9							

Cumulative percentages of marriages which end in divorce

The cumulative percentages of marriages which end in divorce increase more rapidly in the first 10 years of marriage than the 10 years after that. Once the 20th wedding anniversary is reached, the cumulative percentages increase less rapidly

Source: Office for National Statistics ©
Crown copyright 2011
www.ons.gov.uk

SEE ALSO:
Children and divorce: the father's case, pg78, Essential Articles 14
Partners, pg76, Fact File 2011
www.completeissues.co.uk

Man of the house

How happy are couples with their roles within the family?

Stay at home dads

Just over ten years ago only **60,000** men took on the role of the main parent – now at least **1.4 million** do. This amounts to **14%** of UK households with dependent children.

26% of dads either gave up work or reduced their working hours after the birth of their children, and **44%** regularly look after their children while their partner works.

Of men who are the stay-at-home parent:

Feel lucky to have the opportunity to spend so much time with their kids	43%
Find being the main childcare provider makes them feel 'less of a man'	17%
Find looking after children harder than going out to work	13%
Wish they earned more than their partners so they could go out to work	13%
Parenting/working arrangements have caused arguments with their partners	5%

25% of families with children under 18 say the childcare is shared equally between both parents. This is up from **18%** in **2010.**

Breadwinner mums

25% of women said they earn more than their partner, while **16%** said they earn roughly the same.

46% of families said the decision as to who would be the main child carer was based on who earned the most.

SEE ALSO:
Who's busiest, p190

Is the new woman's place in the home? pg196, Essential Articles 14

A woman's place... is in the home, p182, Fact File 2011

www.completeissues.co.uk

Base: 2,000 parents with dependent children

Source: www.aviva.com

Financial issues

Pocket money

What is the right amount of pocket money?

More than 8 in 10 children still receive pocket money each week.

The amount has risen from last year by 36p per week – an extra £18.72 over a year.

Average amount of pocket money, by region

London	£ 7.63
Scotland	£ 6.89
West Midlands	£ 6.49
South East	£ 6.27
North West	£ 6.06
Yorkshire/Humberside	£ 5.96
North East	£ 5.84
East Anglia	£ 5.79
East Midlands	£ 5.62
Wales	£ 5.43
South West	£ 5.15

The average pocket money children received each week in 2011 rose to £6.25 from a seven year low of £5.89 in 2010. The gender gap has also continued to close with boys getting £6.41 per week and girls £6.09 per week – now only a 32p per week gap compared to 40p last year. Girls aged 12 to 15 are only 11p behind boys of the same age, who receive £7.24 per week.

Despite the differences in pocket money between age groups, genders, and regions, 51% believe they receive the right amount but 43% of children think they deserve more money. Overall, girls (53%) are more content with the amount they receive than boys (48%).

Children in Scotland, Yorkshire and Humberside and the West Midlands are most content with 59% happy with the amount they receive.

Average amount of pocket money by age

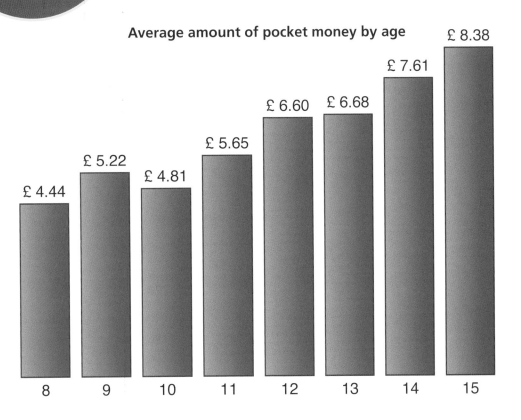

Age	Amount
8	£ 4.44
9	£ 5.22
10	£ 4.81
11	£ 5.65
12	£ 6.60
13	£ 6.68
14	£ 7.61
15	£ 8.38

Base: 1,202 children aged 8-15 across Great Britain

Source: Halifax Pocket Money Survey for 2011
www.halifax.co.uk

SEE ALSO:
www.completeissues.co.uk

100% giving

What made donors open their wallets in 2011?

81p in every pound donated to Oxfam goes directly to programme work to tackle poverty, while 19p is spent on running costs.

Oxfam researched people's attitudes to donating to charity.

They questioned a nationally representative sample of 1,030 British adults.

They found that an important barrier that stops people giving is the thought that part of their donation is going towards running costs.

They also found that people thought more money went towards running costs than is actually true. Most people thought these were 3 times higher than they actually are.

Why do people give?

- It depends what a person thinks of a charity and whether they think they can make a difference by donating

What stops people giving?

- The thought that a significant proportion of their money will not end up getting to those who need it
- the recession and the effect on their own lifestyle that supporting a charity would have

How do they choose?

- Nowadays, there are so many causes to donate to, that people prioritise who and how much they can help.
- Only 14% of those questioned had felt moved by hard-hitting advertising campaigns.

Inclination doesn't always mean action

- People may not necessarily donate if they think that organisations or governments should act first.
- People were also concerned about being asked to do more, and even felt as though they were being taken advantage of.
- In the past, people may have given to charity because they were influenced by other people but now, less than half are motivated by what those close to them will think.

Giving: the numbers

The research showed:

59% of those questioned believe that **a proportion of banker bonuses should go to charities**

8% say if they didn't give to charity **they would feel guilty**

36% feel that technological advances mean it's **easier than before to donate to charity**

65% admit they have been put off supporting charities **because of running costs**

77% of the public believe that **businesses should do more** to help and support charitable organisations

55% say caring about the **cause the charity supports** is the main reason they donate

55% of those questioned thought that giving to charity in 2011 would result in them being **asked to do more and more**

72% of those questioned believe service **running costs eat up a significant part of their donation**

44% put their hand in their wallet because they **want to help**

22% of people believe that the recession has caused them to **think more** about others, but **almost half** of people say that they will donate less money as a result

x5 The over 55s are five times **more likely to be committed to donating to charity than 18–24 year-olds.** Yet the over 55s are most likely to strongly disagree that they have a moral duty to donate to charity

16% donate because it **makes them feel good about themselves**

SEE ALSO:
"I'm giving £1m to charity on an ordinary salary", p88, Essential Articles 14

www.completeissues.co.uk

Source: 100% Giving Report, Oxfam
www.oxfam.org.uk/giving

In it to win it

Nearly three quarters of adults in Britain gamble

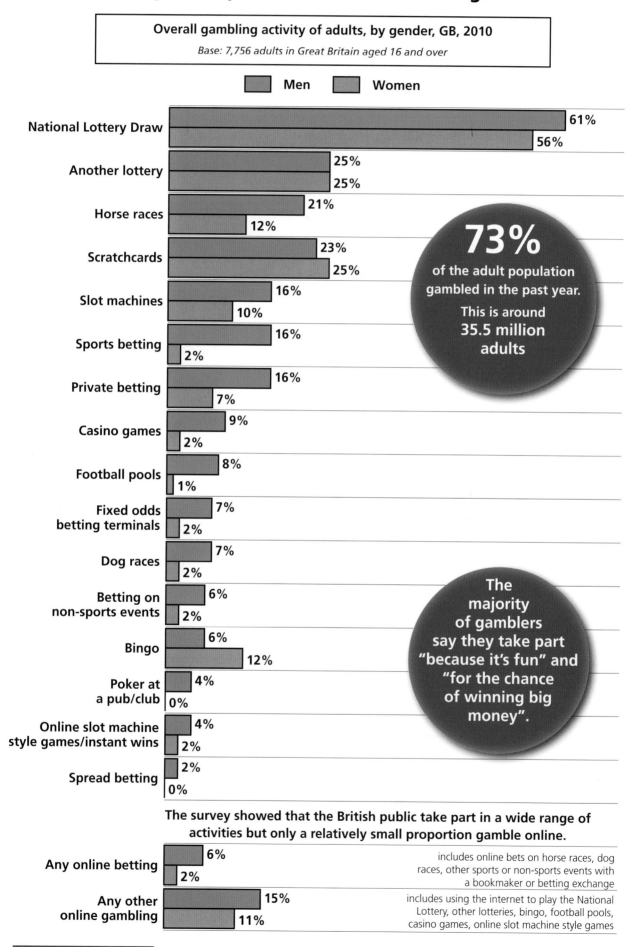

Overall gambling activity of adults, by gender, GB, 2010
Base: 7,756 adults in Great Britain aged 16 and over

■ Men   ☐ Women

Activity	Men	Women
National Lottery Draw	61%	56%
Another lottery	25%	25%
Horse races	21%	12%
Scratchcards	23%	25%
Slot machines	16%	10%
Sports betting	16%	2%
Private betting	16%	7%
Casino games	9%	2%
Football pools	8%	1%
Fixed odds betting terminals	7%	2%
Dog races	7%	2%
Betting on non-sports events	6%	2%
Bingo	6%	12%
Poker at a pub/club	4%	0%
Online slot machine style games/instant wins	4%	2%
Spread betting	2%	0%

73% of the adult population gambled in the past year. This is around **35.5 million adults**

The majority of gamblers say they take part "because it's fun" and "for the chance of winning big money".

The survey showed that the British public take part in a wide range of activities but only a relatively small proportion gamble online.

Any online betting	6% / 2%	includes online bets on horse races, dog races, other sports or non-sports events with a bookmaker or betting exchange
Any other online gambling	15% / 11%	includes using the internet to play the National Lottery, other lotteries, bingo, football pools, casino games, online slot machine style games

When gambling stops being fun...

GamCare provides support, information and advice to anyone suffering from a gambling problem.

GamCare Helpline:
0845 6000 133

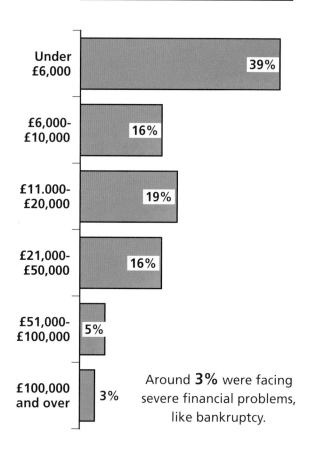

Amount of debt disclosed by callers to GamCare, 2009/10
Base: 1,611 who disclosed debt

Under £6,000	39%
£6,000-£10,000	16%
£11.000-£20,000	19%
£21,000-£50,000	16%
£51,000-£100,000	5%
£100,000 and over	3%

Around **3%** were facing severe financial problems, like bankruptcy.

Most common concerns caused by problem gambling disclosed by callers to GamCare, 2009/10
Base: 16,587

Legend: Gambler | Partner | Family/Friend

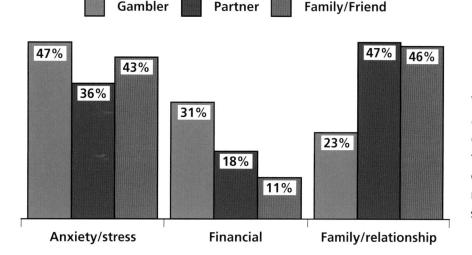

	Gambler	Partner	Family/Friend
Anxiety/stress	47%	36%	43%
Financial	31%	18%	11%
Family/relationship	23%	47%	46%

Attitudes
When people were asked about their attitudes to gambling, most said that there were too many opportunities for gambling nowadays and gambling should be discouraged.

*Sources: Gambling Commission – British Gambling Prevalence Survey 2010 ©
National Centre for Social Research 2011; GamCare Statistics 2009/10
www.gamblingcommission.gov.uk
www.gamcare.org.uk*

SEE ALSO:
www.completeissues.co.uk

Fact File 2012 • www.carelpress.com

Financial issues 73

Deep in debt

We owe more than we earn!

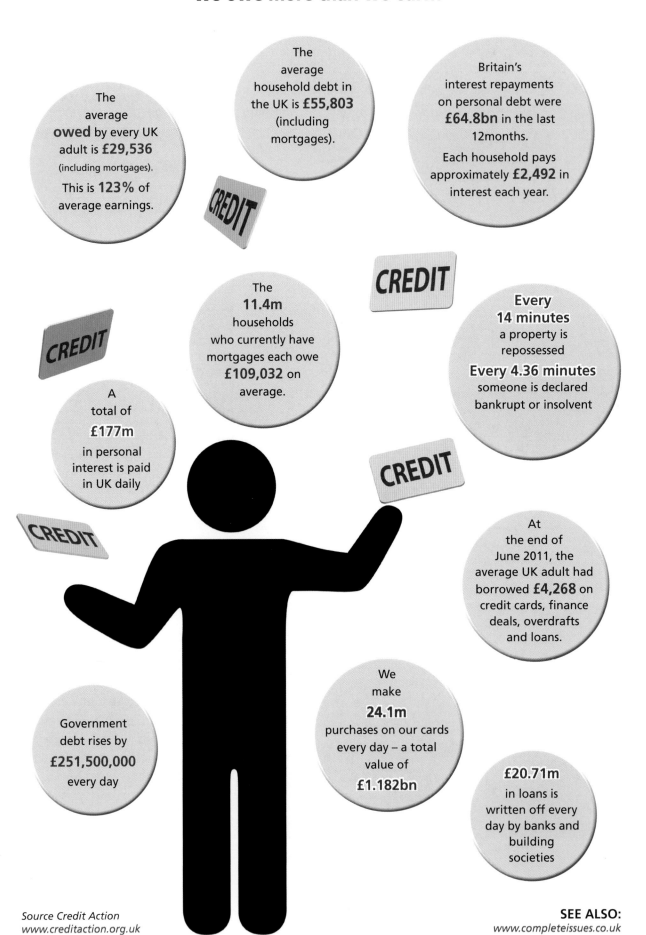

The average **owed** by every UK adult is **£29,536** (including mortgages). This is **123%** of average earnings.

The average household debt in the UK is **£55,803** (including mortgages).

Britain's interest repayments on personal debt were **£64.8bn** in the last 12months. Each household pays approximately **£2,492** in interest each year.

The **11.4m** households who currently have mortgages each owe **£109,032** on average.

Every **14 minutes** a property is repossessed **Every 4.36 minutes** someone is declared bankrupt or insolvent

A total of **£177m** in personal interest is paid in UK daily

At the end of June 2011, the average UK adult had borrowed **£4,268** on credit cards, finance deals, overdrafts and loans.

Government debt rises by **£251,500,000** every day

We make **24.1m** purchases on our cards every day – a total value of **£1.182bn**

£20.71m in loans is written off every day by banks and building societies

CREDIT

Source Credit Action
www.creditaction.org.uk

SEE ALSO:
www.completeissues.co.uk

Debt hotspots

There are large differences in debt between UK regions

In 2010, Consumer Credit Counselling Service – a free debt advice service – reported that the people that called them for help had an average debt of **£19,338** on credit cards, personal loans and other unsecured debt.

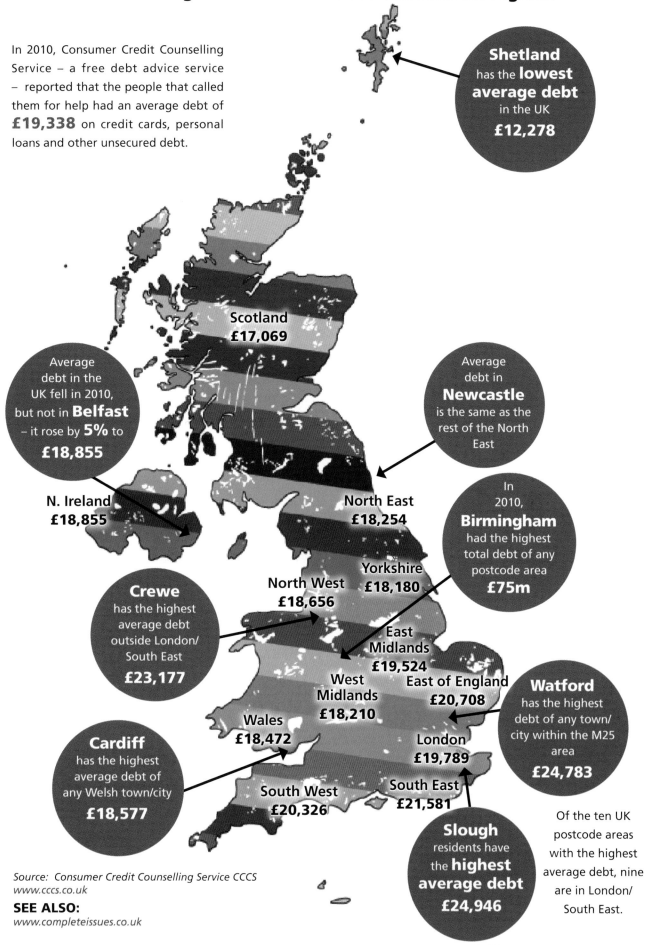

Shetland has the **lowest average debt** in the UK **£12,278**

Scotland **£17,069**

Average debt in the UK fell in 2010, but not in **Belfast** – it rose by **5%** to **£18,855**

Average debt in **Newcastle** is the same as the rest of the North East

N. Ireland **£18,855**

North East **£18,254**

In 2010, **Birmingham** had the highest total debt of any postcode area **£75m**

Yorkshire **£18,180**

North West **£18,656**

Crewe has the highest average debt outside London/ South East **£23,177**

East Midlands **£19,524**

West Midlands **£18,210**

East of England **£20,708**

Watford has the highest debt of any town/ city within the M25 area **£24,783**

Wales **£18,472**

London **£19,789**

Cardiff has the highest average debt of any Welsh town/city **£18,577**

South West **£20,326**

South East **£21,581**

Slough residents have the **highest average debt** **£24,946**

Of the ten UK postcode areas with the highest average debt, nine are in London/ South East.

Source: Consumer Credit Counselling Service CCCS
www.cccs.co.uk

SEE ALSO:
www.completeissues.co.uk

Struggling to save

13% of Britons, 6 million people, have no savings

A survey of 2,597 people in April 2011 gave a
snapshot of how Britain was saving

On average, we set aside
8.31% of our income every month –
approximately **£100.24**

Men set aside more than women –
£115.80 compared to
£84.84

On average men manage to save **8.43%**
of their salary every month compared to
8.19% of women

26% of Britons set themselves a savings goal

Of those **with a savings goal**

32% said they prioritise saving in
case of an emergency

35% were saving for a deposit
to buy a home

37% were saving for a summer holiday

21% were saving for retirement

21% were saving for a car

19% were saving for their
children's future

36% of the population do not believe they have enough money to cope in an emergency

16-24 year olds are
particularly committed to
saving money:

40% set themselves savings
goals compared to only
25% of those aged 35-44.

44% of the younger
generation are more
confident in their ability to
save in the coming months
compared to just **14%** of
the 35-44 year olds.

25% of Britons said they were less likely to save over the following three months

Source: NS&I Savings Survey
www.nsandi.com

SEE ALSO:
Spend or save?, p82, Fact File 2011
www.completeissues.co.uk

Food & drink

Ethical eating

We have concerns about ethical eating, yet we do not act on them

PEOPLE SAY THEY WANT SUSTAINABLE FOOD, BUT WHAT DO THEY MEAN?

There is no legal definition of 'sustainable food,' although some aspects, such as the terms 'organic' or 'Fairtrade', are clearly defined and understood.

Generally sustainable food should be produced, processed and traded in ways that:

- **Contribute** to thriving local economies and sustainable livelihoods.

- **Protect** the diversity of both plants and animals (and the welfare of farmed and wild species), and avoid damaging natural resources and contributing to climate change;

- **Provide** social benefits, such as good quality food, safe and healthy products, and educational opportunities.

How important do you rate the following when shopping for food?

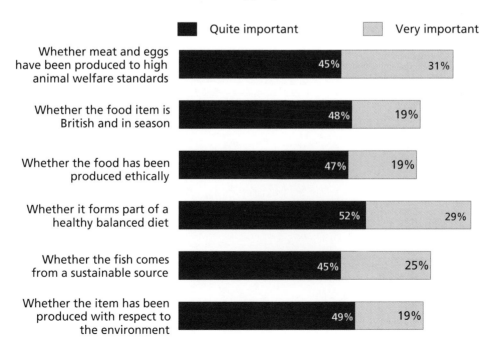

Legend: ■ Quite important   □ Very important

	Quite important	Very important
Whether meat and eggs have been produced to high animal welfare standards	45%	31%
Whether the food item is British and in season	48%	19%
Whether the food has been produced ethically	47%	19%
Whether it forms part of a healthy balanced diet	52%	29%
Whether the fish comes from a sustainable source	45%	25%
Whether the item has been produced with respect to the environment	49%	19%

Which of the following, if any, are on your mind whilst deciding what to buy when you are shopping? Tick all that apply

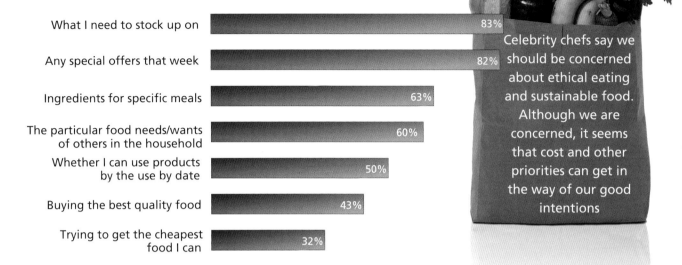

What I need to stock up on	83%
Any special offers that week	82%
Ingredients for specific meals	63%
The particular food needs/wants of others in the household	60%
Whether I can use products by the use by date	50%
Buying the best quality food	43%
Trying to get the cheapest food I can	32%

Celebrity chefs say we should be concerned about ethical eating and sustainable food. Although we are concerned, it seems that cost and other priorities can get in the way of our good intentions

What is of high importance to you and what are you actively seeking to buy?

◼ Higher importance   ◼ Actively seeking to buy

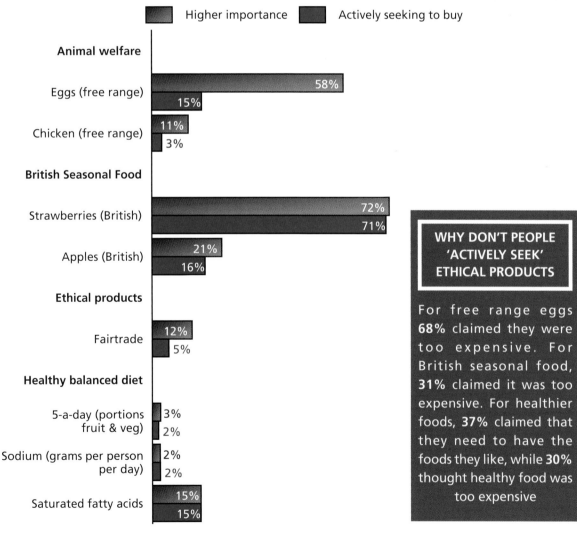

Animal welfare

Eggs (free range) — 58% / 15%

Chicken (free range) — 11% / 3%

British Seasonal Food

Strawberries (British) — 72% / 71%

Apples (British) — 21% / 16%

Ethical products

Fairtrade — 12% / 5%

Healthy balanced diet

5-a-day (portions fruit & veg) — 3% / 2%

Sodium (grams per person per day) — 2% / 2%

Saturated fatty acids — 15% / 15%

WHY DON'T PEOPLE 'ACTIVELY SEEK' ETHICAL PRODUCTS

For free range eggs **68%** claimed they were too expensive. For British seasonal food, **31%** claimed it was too expensive. For healthier foods, **37%** claimed that they need to have the foods they like, while **30%** thought healthy food was too expensive

Source: Attitudes and Behaviours around Sustainable Food Purchasing, April 2011, DEFRA © Crown copyright 2011
www.defra.gov.uk
www.sustainweb.org

SEE ALSO:
www.completeissues.co.uk

Organic market

Although shoppers would like to buy organic food, they are also feeling the economic pinch

Sales of organic products fell by 5.9% to £1.73 billion in 2010 according to the Organic Market Report

Annual organic sales figures 2001-2010
(£ millions)

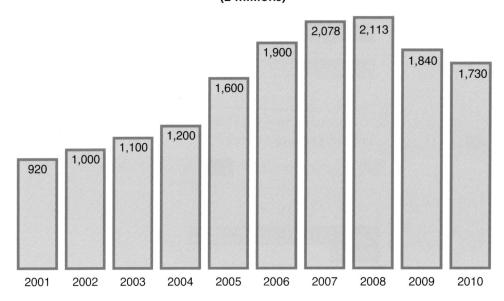

Year	Sales
2001	920
2002	1,000
2003	1,100
2004	1,200
2005	1,600
2006	1,900
2007	2,078
2008	2,113
2009	1,840
2010	1,730

Top reasons for buying organic

Fewer chemicals
65%

Healthier for me/my family
55%

Natural/unprocessed
54%

Better for nature/the environment
46%

Kinder to animals
44%

Tastes better
40%

Safer to eat
39%

More ethical
36%

No GM ingredients
28%

Organic appeal:

Organic food and drink seems to have a broad appeal, with 17 out of 20 households (86%) buying some organic products in 2010. But on average consumers only bought organic products 15 times during the year, compared to 16 times in 2009.

Our budget & our food:

A combination of low wages , higher food-prices and rising unemployment is squeezing family budgets.

The proportion of our income that we spent on food was at an all-time low of 8.6% in 2006. However, recently it has edged up to almost 10%.

How has this affected the organic market?

In the organic sector the squeeze on family budgets shows in the way some shoppers have 'traded down' to less expensive options. Organic eggs are now 3.5% of the egg market, compared to 5.5% two years ago. Demand for organic mince and stewing beef grew in 2010, while sales of joints and steaks fell. Despite our other concerns, it seems we put cost first.

What shoppers said...

I choose the most affordable food
75%

I really care about the origin of my food
67%

I care passionately about environmental issues
67%

I'm happy to pay more for the best quality
65%

I always buy organic food
35%

Source: Soil Association Organic Market Report 2011
www.soilassociation.org

SEE ALSO:
www.completeissues.co.uk

Time to eat

Although most parents were happy with their child's school meal arrangements they wanted to see some improvements

79.8% of parents were moderately or completely **happy** with the lunchtime arrangements for eating at their child's school, **16.4%** were **concerned** and **3.8%** were **very unhappy.**

62.6% of parents said their child's school had a **packed lunch policy** which banned certain food and drinks – **67.8%** agreed with the policy.

What does your child have for lunch?
(percentages do not add up to 100% due to rounding)

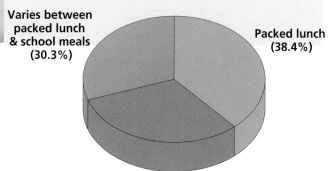

Varies between packed lunch & school meals (30.3%)

Packed lunch (38.4%)

School meals (31.2%)

Would you like your school to improve their lunches in the following ways?
(more than one answer could be ticked)

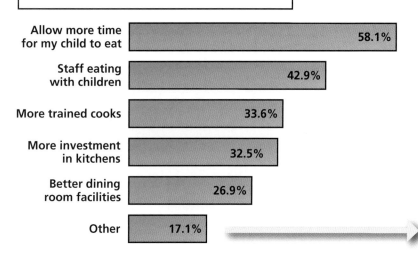

Allow more time for my child to eat	58.1%
Staff eating with children	42.9%
More trained cooks	33.6%
More investment in kitchens	32.5%
Better dining room facilities	26.9%
Other	17.1%

Some **other** answers given were:

- *check with the children to see what they think about their meals and give them a menu choice as they do in hospitals the day before*

- *food prepared and cooked in the school kitchen*

- *all ingredients to be in a school recipe folder in a place where it could be easily viewed*

Only **29%** of parents stated that their child had grumbled about the food.

What are your child's biggest grumbles about eating school lunch?
(more than one answer could be given)

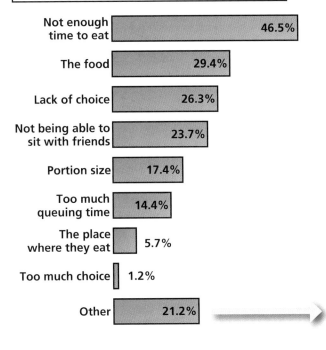

Not enough time to eat	46.5%
The food	29.4%
Lack of choice	26.3%
Not being able to sit with friends	23.7%
Portion size	17.4%
Too much queuing time	14.4%
The place where they eat	5.7%
Too much choice	1.2%
Other	21.2%

Some **other** grumbles were:

- *Not being able to change food choice if they did not like what they had chosen once they have tasted it*
- *having to eat in silence*
- *having a poor menu choice in the 2nd sitting*
- *bossy dinner ladies who don't listen*

What are your biggest concerns about school lunch?
(more than one answer could be given)

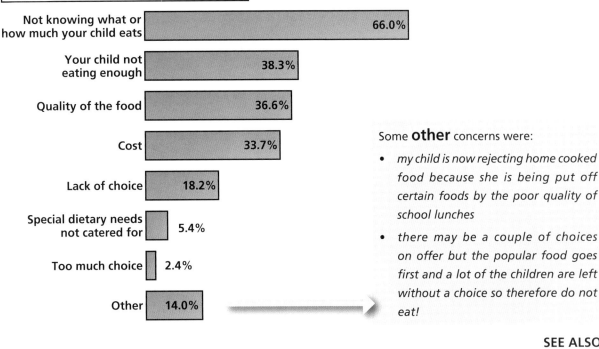

Not knowing what or how much your child eats	66.0%
Your child not eating enough	38.3%
Quality of the food	36.6%
Cost	33.7%
Lack of choice	18.2%
Special dietary needs not catered for	5.4%
Too much choice	2.4%
Other	14.0%

Some **other** concerns were:

- *my child is now rejecting home cooked food because she is being put off certain foods by the poor quality of school lunches*
- *there may be a couple of choices on offer but the popular food goes first and a lot of the children are left without a choice so therefore do not eat!*

SEE ALSO:
If Jamie Oliver can't change our eating habits... who can? p92, Essential Articles 13
Boxing stupid over children's packed lunches, p94, Essential Articles 13
School dinners, p93, Fact File 2011

Base: 2,130 parents

Source: Netmums School Food Survey in conjunction with Parents for better food in schools
www.netmums.com

www.completeissues.co.uk

Calorie conscious

Over half of us do not know how many calories we are consuming when we eat out

What are calories?

Calories are a measure of how much energy food or drink contains. The amount of energy you need will depend on:

your age: eg growing children and teenagers may need more energy

your lifestyle: eg how active you are

your size: height and weight can affect how quickly you use energy

An average **man** needs around **2,500** calories a day to maintain his weight.

For an average **woman**, that figure is around **2,000** calories a day.

With one in six meals eaten outside of the home, the Department of Health is asking restaurants, pubs, cafes, fast food outlets and food retailers to sign up to display calories on menus and menu boards so that consumers can make healthier choices.

34 food organisations have signed up, including McDonald's, Wimpy, KFC, Harvester and Pizza Hut. This means that consumers should be able to see how many calories are in their favourite burger, pizza, salad or muffin by glancing at a menu or menu board.

However, an American study has discovered that displaying calorie contents fails to stop people eating unhealthily. Even though customers became more aware of how much they were eating, it had little effect on what they purchased. Price and taste were more important than any desire to be healthy.

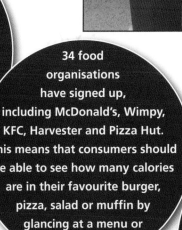

The findings come against a backdrop of the UK having the highest obesity rates in Europe and diet related illnesses costing the NHS £6 billion each year

SEE ALSO:

Why latest diet and calorie news from scientists has me praising the lard for an extra pie, p87, Essential Articles 13

Which fast food meals are the healthiest? Anyone's guess! p114, Essential Articles 12

Cost of 100 calories, p84, Fact File 2010

www.completeissues.co.uk

How many calories do you think are in each of these meals eaten outside of the home (eg pub/restaurant/cafe)?

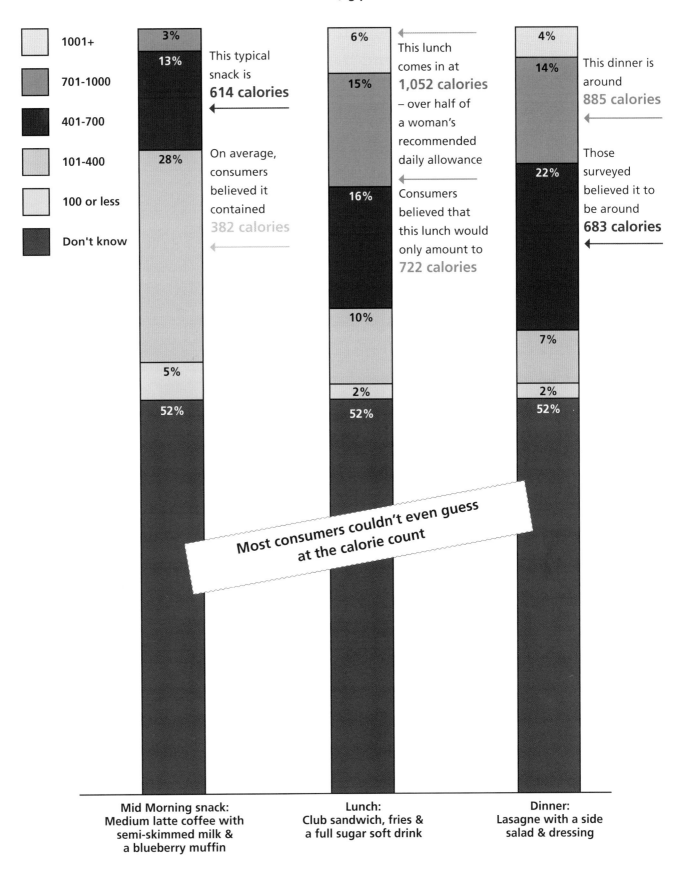

Legend:
- 1001+
- 701-1000
- 401-700
- 101-400
- 100 or less
- Don't know

Mid Morning snack (first bar):
- 3%
- 13%
- 28%
- 5%
- 52%

This typical snack is **614 calories**

On average, consumers believed it contained 382 calories

Lunch (second bar):
- 6%
- 15%
- 16%
- 10%
- 2%
- 52%

This lunch comes in at **1,052 calories** – over half of a woman's recommended daily allowance

Consumers believed that this lunch would only amount to 722 calories

Dinner (third bar):
- 4%
- 14%
- 22%
- 7%
- 2%
- 52%

This dinner is around **885 calories**

Those surveyed believed it to be around **683 calories**

Most consumers couldn't even guess at the calorie count

Mid Morning snack:
Medium latte coffee with semi-skimmed milk & a blueberry muffin

Lunch:
Club sandwich, fries & a full sugar soft drink

Dinner:
Lasagne with a side salad & dressing

Will this change the choices you make?

Source: Calorie Poll, Comres, NHS
www.comres.co.uk
www.bbc.co.uk/news
www.nhs.uk

Base: 1,734 adult consumers, England

Keep calm and bake

Whether it's cupcakes or Cordon Bleu, home baking has boomed during the recession

Baking mad Brits

Consumers have been bitten by the baking bug, as today, **28%** of Brits are baking from scratch using raw ingredients at least once a week. In fact, **69%** of all consumers have bought some kind of baking ingredient in the last year. Only **19%** of consumers say baking from scratch takes too much time.

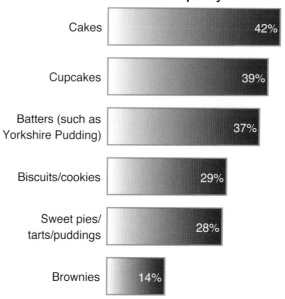

Top items people baked at home in the past year

Item	Percentage
Cakes	42%
Cupcakes	39%
Batters (such as Yorkshire Pudding)	37%
Biscuits/cookies	29%
Sweet pies/tarts/puddings	28%
Brownies	14%

Be thrifty and bake

And we're even finding cheaper means of finding our recipes as **52%** of Brits now get recipe ideas online compared to the **46%** who rely on cookbooks. The importance of the internet for recipes has been driven in part by TV cookery shows and the celebrity chef boom - recipes from the programmes are often available online immediately while books take longer to come out.

In fact, with tightening budgets and relatively less disposable income, **50%** of UK consumers now say they are baking at home as it enables them to cut down on their personal shopping bills.

It seems that while we are saving money, we also like to show off. Nearly half **(45%)** of Brits say they like to showcase their baking skills to friends and family.

Source: Mintel
www.mintel.com

SEE ALSO:
www.completeissues.co.uk

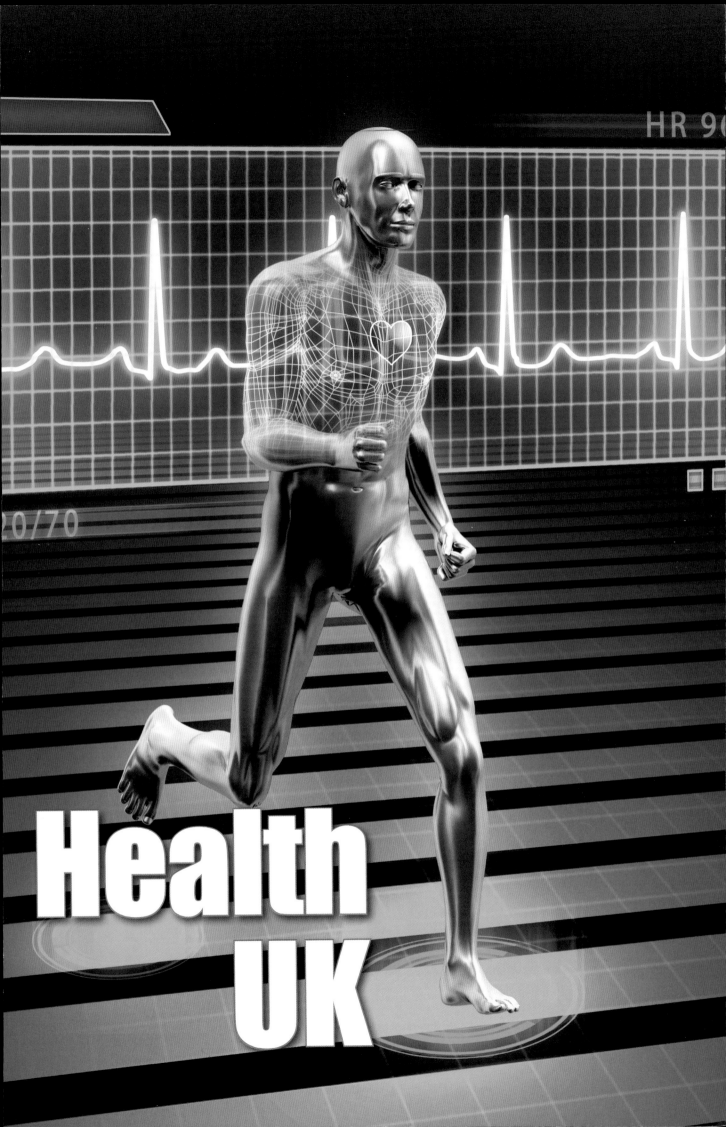

HR 90

20/70

Health
UK

Eating disorders

Young women aged between 10 and 24 are the group most frequently admitted to hospital for an eating disorder

Eating disorders include a range of conditions that can affect someone not only physically but can also affect their mental state and their ability to interact with others.

A person with an eating disorder will appear to have an abnormal attitude towards food, which will affect their behaviour and eating habits.

People suffering with an eating disorder such as anorexia or bulimia, may focus excessively on their weight, body shape, and image. This causes them to make unhealthy choices about food which can have damaging results to their health.

Between July 2009 and June 2010 there were 2,067 people admitted to hospital for all eating disorders. However, there were **2,579** Finished Consultant Episodes (FCEs), an increase of **11%** on the previous year.

An FCE is a period of care in hospital. Figures do not represent the number of different patients, as a person may have more than one episode of care in the same year.

2,326 (90%) of the FCEs were female.

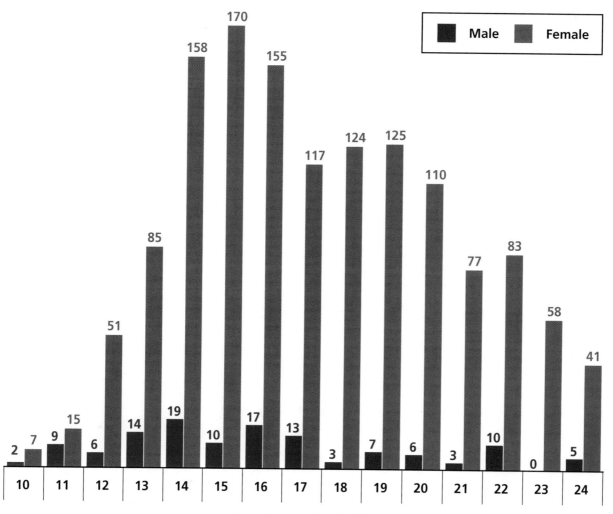

FCEs for eating disorders in 10 to 24 year olds July 2009-June 2010

Legend: Male, Female

Age	10	11	12	13	14	15	16	17	18	19	20	21	22	23	24
Male	2	9	6	14	19	10	17	13	3	7	6	3	10	0	5
Female	7	15	51	85	158	170	155	117	124	125	110	77	83	58	41

Age at start of episode

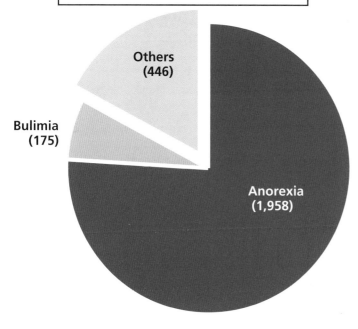

FCEs for eating disorders by type – July 2009 to June 2010

Others (446)

Bulimia (175)

Anorexia (1,958)

	17 or under	18 and over
Anorexia: when someone tries to keep their weight as low as possible, eg by starving themselves or exercising	710	1,247
Bulimia: when someone tries to control their weight by binge eating and then deliberately being sick or using laxatives	15	160
Other: includes overeating or vomiting associated with psychological disturbances, as well as other unspecified eating disorders.	157	287

Admissions to hospitals are much higher for **anorexia** than **bulimia**.

However, **bulimia** is around five times more common than **anorexia**.

90% of people with **bulimia** are female. It usually develops around the age of 18 or 19.

NB groups may not sum to the total in the pie as the figures exclude FCEs where age unknown

"Anyone can develop an eating disorder, regardless of age, sex or cultural or racial background. But the people most likely to be affected tend to be young women, particularly between the ages of 15 and 25"

NHS Choices

SEE ALSO:
Boy's don't cry, p34, Essential Articles 14
What should I do about my overweight niece?
p36, Essential Articles 14
www.completeissues.co.uk

Source: HES online Hospital Episode Statistics – Month 4 Topic of Interest – Eating Disorders www.hesonline.nhs.uk

Visible difference

Despite the recession, the public's interest in cosmetic surgery was still strong in 2010

The British Association of Aesthetic Plastic Surgeons (BAAPS) said that the largest increase in cosmetic surgery in 2010 was on the most visible areas of the body.

Surgeries that decreased in popularity were on areas which could potentially be 'hidden' or disguised by fashion and hairstyles, such as tummy tucks – **down 7.5%** and pinning back prominent ears – **down 17%**

38,274

surgical procedures were carried out by BAAPS members in 2010 – a **5% increase** on 2009

Top surgical procedures for men and women in 2010
(in order of popularity)

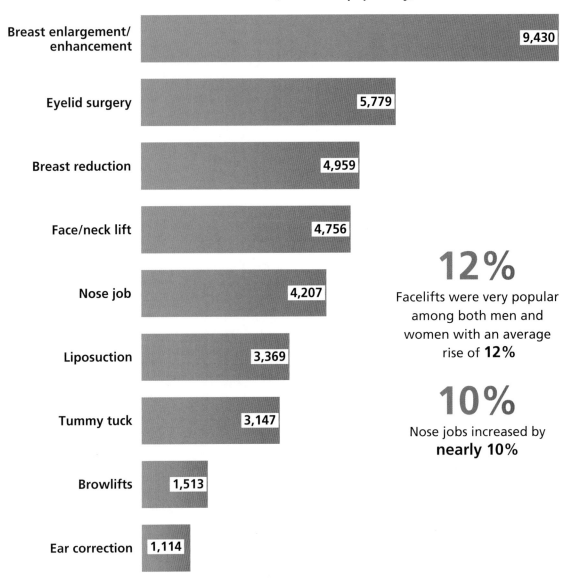

Procedure	Number
Breast enlargement/enhancement	9,430
Eyelid surgery	5,779
Breast reduction	4,959
Face/neck lift	4,756
Nose job	4,207
Liposuction	3,369
Tummy tuck	3,147
Browlifts	1,513
Ear correction	1,114

12%

Facelifts were very popular among both men and women with an average rise of **12%**

10%

Nose jobs increased by **nearly 10%**

Women

Surgery (in order of popularity)	Number of Procedures	% rise or fall from 2009
Breast enlargement/ enhancement	9,418	+10.3%
Eyelid surgery	5,127	+7%
Face/neck lift	4,493	+12%
Breast reduction	4,218	+2.3%
Nose job	3,214	+8.6%
Tummy tuck	3,039	-7%
Liposuction	2,896	-3.8%
Brow lifts	1,390	+5%
Ear correction	618	-23%

34,413
Women had **90%** of all cosmetic procedures in 2010

Men

Surgery (in order of popularity)	Number of Procedures	% rise or fall from 2009
Nose job	993	+13.2%
Breast reduction	741	+27.5%
Eyelid surgery	652	+5.8%
Ear correction	496	-27%
Liposuction	473	+5.2%
Face/neck lift	263	+11.4%
Brow lifts	123	+12.8%
Tummy tuck	108	-20%

3,861
Men had **10%** of all cosmetic procedures in 2010

28%
'man boob' operations are now the 2nd most common procedure among men, rising **28%** over the 2009 figure

SEE ALSO:
Buy now – pay the real price later! p29, Essential Articles 14
www.completeissues.co.uk

Source: The British Association of Aesthetic Plastic Surgeons (BAAP)
www.baaps.org.uk

Sting in the tale

It is hard to prevent insect stings but why aren't we reducing the number of dog bites?

Figures from the NHS Information Centre show that general admissions increased by only 1.8% but admissions for bites, strikes and stings rode by 9.6%. Of the 12,409 admissions for such things, nearly half (6,118) were bites or strikes by dogs.

Number and % of admissions for bites, strikes or stings (May 2010 to April 2011)

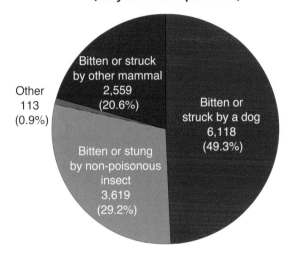

- Other 113 (0.9%)
- Bitten or struck by other mammal 2,559 (20.6%)
- Bitten or stung by non-poisonous insect 3,619 (29.2%)
- Bitten or struck by a dog 6,118 (49.3%)

Who?
Dog bites are most common in young children, particularly boys, who are five to nine years of age. It is estimated that around half of all children will be bitten by a dog at some point during their life. The dog involved is usually either a family dog or a dog that belongs to a friend or neighbour.

Why?
It is thought the main reasons that dogs bite include possessiveness, fear, pain, maternal instinct and hunter drive.

What can we do?
Sheila Merrill, public health adviser for the Royal Society for the Prevention of Accidents (RoSPA), said: "Owners are responsible for making sure that their pet does not pose a risk to other people. That means making sure that the animal is properly trained and restrained - where appropriate - and understanding what causes the animal to feel stressed.

"However placid you think your pet is you should never leave it alone with a small child."

A seasonal trend in the number of insect bites can be seen. This is to be expected as there are more stinging insects around during the warmer months.

Avoiding insects bites and stings is really quite difficult, which makes the increased number of dog bites even more alarming – as so many could be avoided.

Number of admissions by type of bite, strike or sting and month

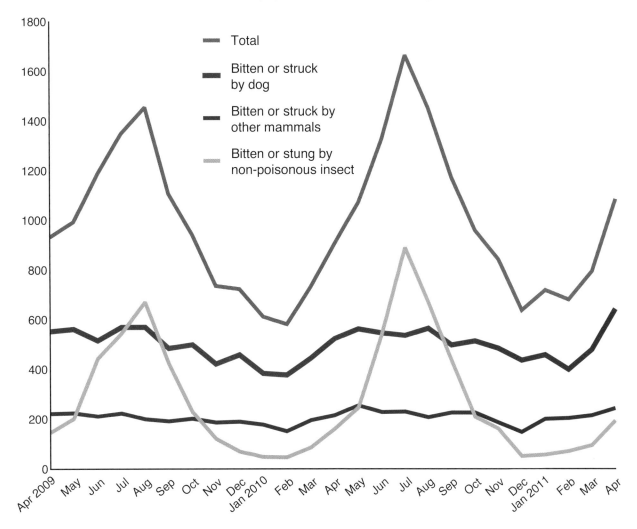

Legend:
- Total
- Bitten or struck by dog
- Bitten or struck by other mammals
- Bitten or stung by non-poisonous insect

SEE ALSO:
In defence of devil dogs, p32, Essential Articles 13

Source: HES Online
www.hesonline.nhs.uk

www.completeissues.co.uk

Common cancers

An estimated 39% of 12 of the most common cancers in the UK could be prevented

Estimated **percentage** of cancer types which could be **prevented** per year, just through healthy changes in diet, physical activity and weight. This doesn't take into account other major risk factors such as smoking and sun damage.

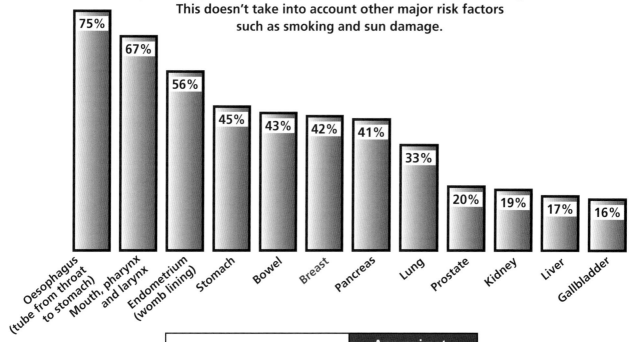

Type of cancer	Approximate **number** of cases per year that could be **prevented**
Breast	19,200
Bowel	16,600
Lung	13,000
Prostate	7,200
Oesophagus	6,000
Mouth, pharynx and larynx	5,100
Endometrium	4,200
Stomach	3,500
Pancreas	3,150
Kidney	1,600
Liver	580
Gallbladder	120

NB Rates have been adjusted to take account of the different age ranges of different populations in different countries

12,068 women died of breast cancer in the UK in 2008.

Scientists estimate about **42%** of breast cancer cases in the UK could be prevented through maintaining a healthy weight, drinking less alcohol and being more physically active. It is also thought that breastfeeding reduces the risk of breast cancer.

In other parts of the world, where the lifestyle is very different, the rate is different. For example, women in Eastern Africa drink much less alcohol than women in the UK and obesity levels are much lower. Breastfeeding rates in Eastern Africa are also much higher.

The **UK** has the **joint 9th** highest breast cancer rate – **four times** higher than those in Eastern Africa.

In the UK there were **89 women per 100,000** diagnosed with cancer in 2008, compared to **19.3 women per 100,000**, in Eastern Africa.

However, these figures can be affected by better diagnosis and recording of breast cancer cases in the UK.

"The fact that breast cancer rates in Eastern Africa are so much lower than in the UK is a stark reminder that every year in this country, thousands of women are diagnosed with a case of cancer that could have been prevented."

Dr Rachel Thompson, Deputy Head of Science for WCRF

SEE ALSO:
The big killers: Cancer, p104
www.completeissues.co.uk

Source: World Cancer Research Fund
www.wcrf-uk.org

HIV UK

UK-acquired HIV has nearly doubled over the past decade

Each year, many thousands of individuals are diagnosed with HIV for the first time.

There is often a lengthy 'silent' period before HIV is diagnosed because people are afraid of the stigma.

Late diagnosis severely affects the health prospects of people with HIV.

On average, of all those who die from HIV infection every year, **three out of five** are diagnosed late – that is after the point their treatment should have begun.

New drugs and therapies have brought about large reductions in cases of AIDS and in deaths from it in the UK.

New diagnoses in men who have sex with men have increased by **70%** in the past ten years rising from **1,810** in 2001 to **3,080** in 2010.

The number of new diagnoses among heterosexuals infected abroad continues to fall, largely due to a decrease in diagnoses among persons from sub-Saharan Africa.

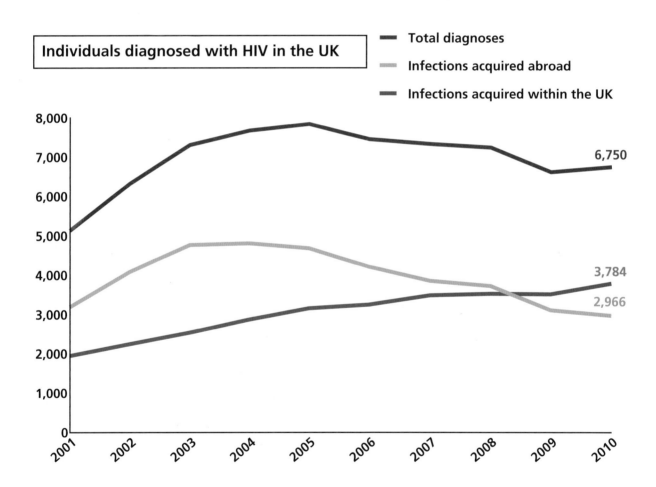

Individuals diagnosed with HIV in the UK

— Total diagnoses
— Infections acquired abroad
— Infections acquired within the UK

...in the last few years, new diagnoses of HIV infections acquired within the UK are on the upward turn, especially in men who have sex with men...

Dr Paul Cosford, executive director of Health Protection Services, Health Protection Agency

Numbers of new HIV diagnoses, by gender, 2010

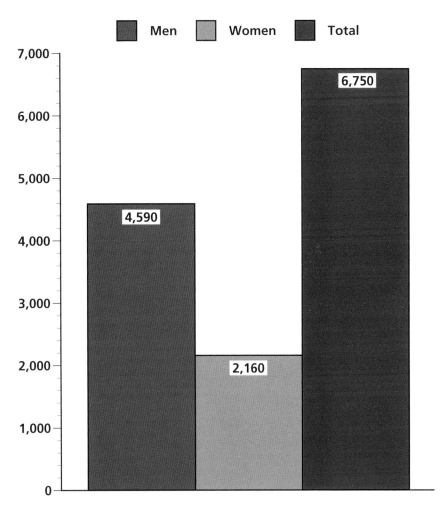

Men   Women   Total

- 7,000
- 6,000
- 5,000
- 4,000
- 3,000
- 2,000
- 1,000
- 0

4,590

2,160

6,750

The total of new diagnoses represents a rate of

15.7

per 100,000 population aged 15 to 59.

For **men** this is

21.4

per 100,000

For women

10.1

per 100,000

New diagnoses for people infected with HIV in the UK increased from

1,950

in 2001 to

3,780

in 2010

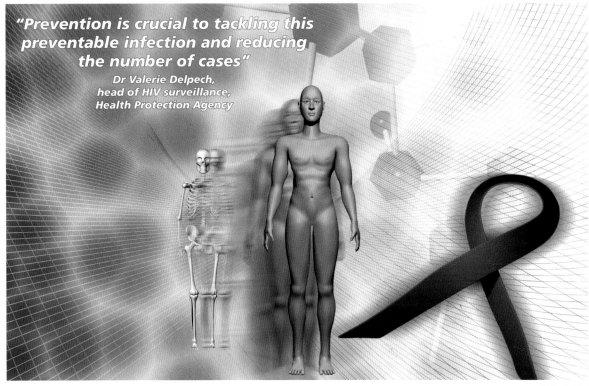

"Prevention is crucial to tackling this preventable infection and reducing the number of cases"

*Dr Valerie Delpech,
head of HIV surveillance,
Health Protection Agency*

SEE ALSO:
Living with HIV, p108
Dying of AIDS, p110
Sexfactor, p108, Fact File 2010
www.completeissues.co.uk

Source: Health Protection Agency
www.hpa.org.uk

TB in the UK

Tuberculosis cases have risen in the UK to over 9,000 – the highest number for nearly 30 years

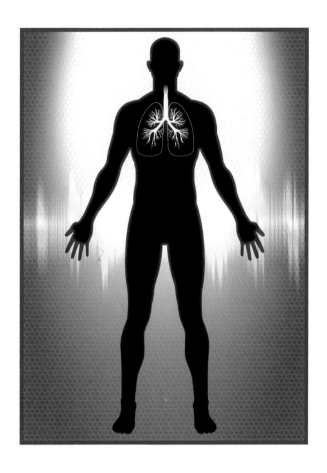

What is TB?

TB is a bacterial infection spread by the coughs or sneezes of an infected person.

The bacteria responsible for TB are very slow moving, so a person may not experience any symptoms for many months, or even years, after becoming infected.

TB can affect anyone. The bacteria can attack any part of the body, but most commonly the lungs.

Before antibiotics, TB used to be a major health problem, but by the 1980s, TB was thought to be almost wiped out in the UK.

However, in recent years TB cases have been increasing – in part due to the increase in travel and migration.

Who does it affect?

TB is particularly common among:

- people living in urban areas (like many other infectious diseases);
- people who come from countries where TB is widespread;
- people living in areas of deprivation where their health and nutrition are poor;
- homeless people and drug users who may not have easy access to healthcare services;
- people who have HIV.

Most cases of TB occur in major cities.

38% of cases were in London – rates in some parts of the region are over **80 per 100,000,** similar to those reported in some high incidence countries in South America, Asia and North Africa.

The North East region had the fewest cases – just **2%.**

55% of all TB cases in 2009 were male. Cases in patients under 15 years of age, however, were more likely to be female – **53%.**

> "Poor housing, inadequate ventilation and overcrowding, conditions that were prevalent in Victorian Britain a century ago, are causes of the higher TB incidence rates in certain London boroughs"
> *Professor Alimuddin Zumla of University College London*

The increase in the number of TB cases in the UK has largely been in non-UK born groups.

In 2009, these included black African **28%**, Indian **27%**, and white people **10%**.

However, **85%** of individuals born overseas were not recent immigrants.

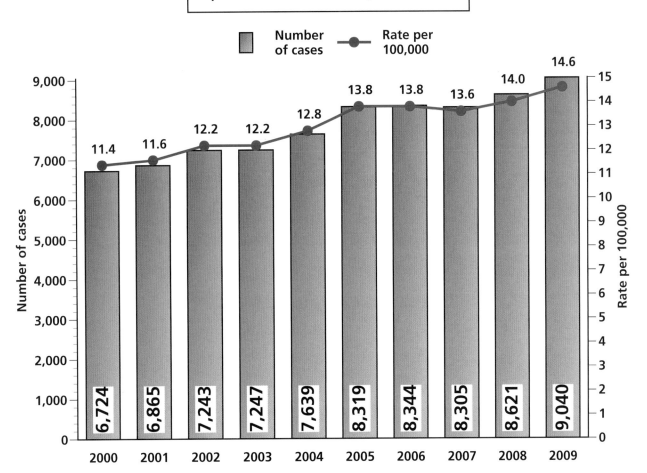

Reported TB cases and rates, UK 2000-2009

Number of cases | Rate per 100,000

Year	Number of cases	Rate per 100,000
2000	6,724	11.4
2001	6,865	11.6
2002	7,243	12.2
2003	7,247	12.2
2004	7,639	12.8
2005	8,319	13.8
2006	8,344	13.8
2007	8,305	13.6
2008	8,621	14.0
2009	9,040	14.6

As the current figures are only for reported cases, the true disease prevalence may be even higher

Prevention and cure

The BCG vaccine provides effective protection against TB in up to 8 out of 10 of people who are given it.

BCG vaccinations are not routinely given as part of the childhood vaccination schedule, unless a baby is thought to have a higher than normal risk of coming into contact with TB.

For example, babies born in areas of inner-city London, where TB rates are higher than in the rest of the country, will probably be given the BCG vaccination.

With treatment, a TB infection can usually be cured.

Most people will need to take a long-term course of antibiotics, which usually lasts for at least six months.

Source: Tuberculosis in the UK: Annual report on tuberculosis surveillance in the UK, 2010 – Health Protection Agency Centre for Infections. NHS Choices Health News December 2010
www.hpa.org.uk
www.nhs.uk/news

SEE ALSO:
Global TB, p106
TB: 'I was a medical mystery', p120, Essential Articles 14
www.completeissues.co.uk

Malaria in the UK

Malaria is a potentially deadly disease but is almost completely preventable

Dr Jane Jones, Head of the Health Protection Agency's travel and migrant health section

There is no risk of catching malaria in the UK but travellers to countries where it is a problem, eg in Africa, South and Central America, Asia and the Middle East, need to take precautions in order to prevent infection.

Over the last ten years, around **half** of all cases of malaria reported in the UK have been seen in people who travel to West Africa and India, mostly to visit friends and relatives.

This group of people may be more likely to acquire malaria for a number of reasons including:

- not getting medical advice on malaria prevention before travel;

- receiving poor advice or not taking advice;

- not realising that they might be at risk, because the destination is familiar to them

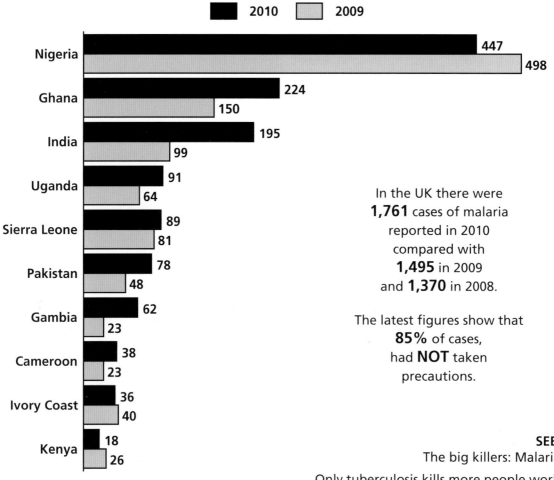

UK malaria cases per country of infection

■ 2010   □ 2009

Nigeria: 447 (2010), 498 (2009)
Ghana: 224 (2010), 150 (2009)
India: 195 (2010), 99 (2009)
Uganda: 91 (2010), 64 (2009)
Sierra Leone: 89 (2010), 81 (2009)
Pakistan: 78 (2010), 48 (2009)
Gambia: 62 (2010), 23 (2009)
Cameroon: 38 (2010), 23 (2009)
Ivory Coast: 36 (2010), 40 (2009)
Kenya: 18 (2010), 26 (2009)

In the UK there were **1,761** cases of malaria reported in 2010 compared with **1,495** in 2009 and **1,370** in 2008.

The latest figures show that **85%** of cases, had **NOT** taken precautions.

SEE ALSO:
The big killers: Malaria, p102
Only tuberculosis kills more people worldwide, see Global TB, p106 and TB in the UK, p98

Source: Health Protection Agency
www.hpa.org.uk

www.completeissues.co.uk

Fact File 2012 • www.carelpress.com

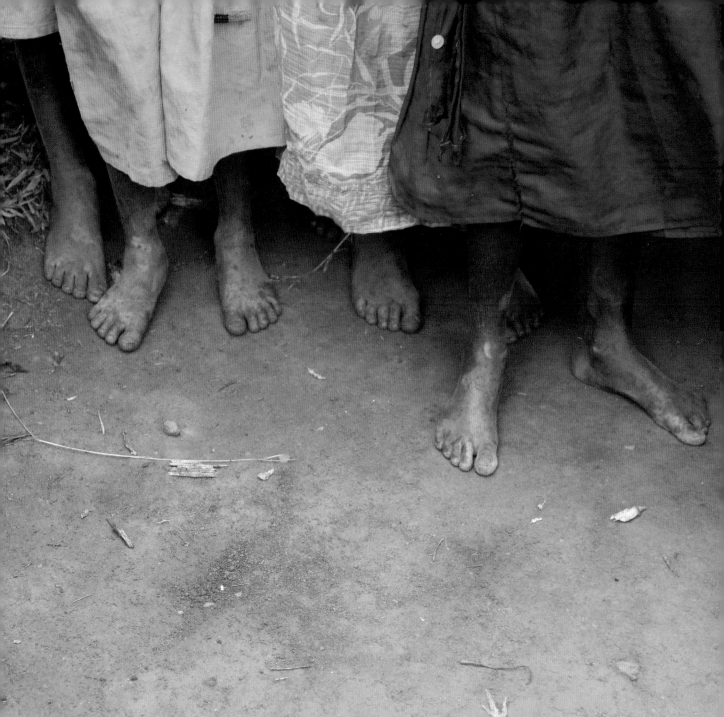

Health
worldwide

The big killers: Malaria

About 3.3 billion people – half of the world's population – are at risk of malaria

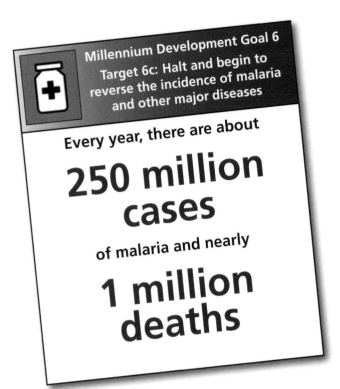

Millennium Development Goal 6

Target 6c: Halt and begin to reverse the incidence of malaria and other major diseases

Every year, there are about

250 million cases

of malaria and nearly

1 million deaths

Malaria is caused by a parasite which is transmitted through the bites of infected mosquitoes.

If not treated promptly with effective medicines, malaria can often be fatal.

Some ways to control malaria include:

- prompt and effective treatment;
- use of mosquito nets treated with insecticide;
- indoor spraying with insecticide

People living in the poorest countries are the most vulnerable to malaria.

In many parts of the world the parasites have developed resistance to some malaria medicines.

Number of cases per WHO region 2000 & 2009

WHO regions	2000	2009
African	173m	176m
Americas	2.8m	1.1m
Eastern Mediterranean	15m	12m
European	47,000	1,000
South-East Asia	38m	34m
Western Pacific	2.8m	2.3m
World	233m	225m

Malaria cases peaked at 244m in 2005. The largest percentage reductions since 2005 were in the **European region** – **86%** – followed by the **Americas** – **42%**. In **Africa** the reduction was less than **10%**.

Percentage of malaria cases worldwide 2009

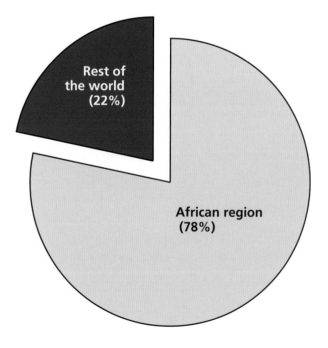

Rest of the world (22%)

African region (78%)

Number of **deaths** per WHO region 2000 & 2009

WHO regions	2000	2009
African	900,000	709,000
Americas	2,400	1,300
Eastern Mediterranean	18,000	16,000
European	0	0
South-East Asia	58,000	49,000
Western Pacific	6,000	5,300
World	985,000	781,000

The largest percentage decrease since 2000 was seen in the **Americas – 48%** – but the largest actual decline was seen in the **African region** – by **193,000.**

However, Africa still accounted for **91%** of deaths.

About **85%** of deaths in 2009 were in children under 5 years of age.

Over the past decade, a new group of drugs has brought new hope in the fight against malaria

Source: World Malaria Report 2010 © WHO
www.who.int/features/factfiles/malaria/en/index.html
www.undp.org/mdg/goal6.shtml

Percentage of malaria **deaths** worldwide 2009

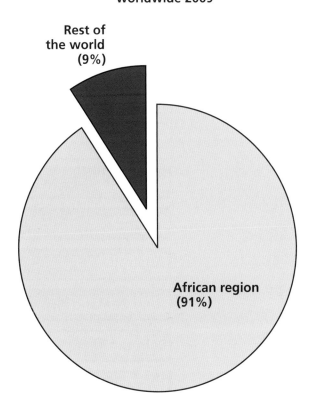

Rest of the world (9%)

African region (91%)

Every 30 seconds a child dies from malaria

Pregnant women are at high risk not only of dying from the complications of severe malaria, but also spontaneous abortion, premature delivery or stillbirth.

Malaria contributes to the deaths of an estimated 10,000 pregnant women and up to 200,000 infants each year in Africa alone.

SEE ALSO:
Malaria in the UK, p100

Only tuberculosis kills more people worldwide, see Global TB, p106 and TB in the UK, p98
www.completeissues.co.uk

The big killers: Cancer

There are an estimated 12.7 million cancer cases around the world every year. By 2030 there could be 26 million cases

Ten highest overall cancer rates in the world, per 100,000 people

Denmark	326
Ireland	317
Australia	314
New Zealand	309
Belgium	307
France	300
USA	300
Norway	299
Canada	297
Czech Republic	295

The **UK** has the **22nd** highest cancer rate

UK	267

Cancer mortality

In the **UK** in 2008, there were

156,594

cancer deaths.

Of these deaths,

81,587

were **men** and

75,007

were **women**

Highest cancer rates for men and women

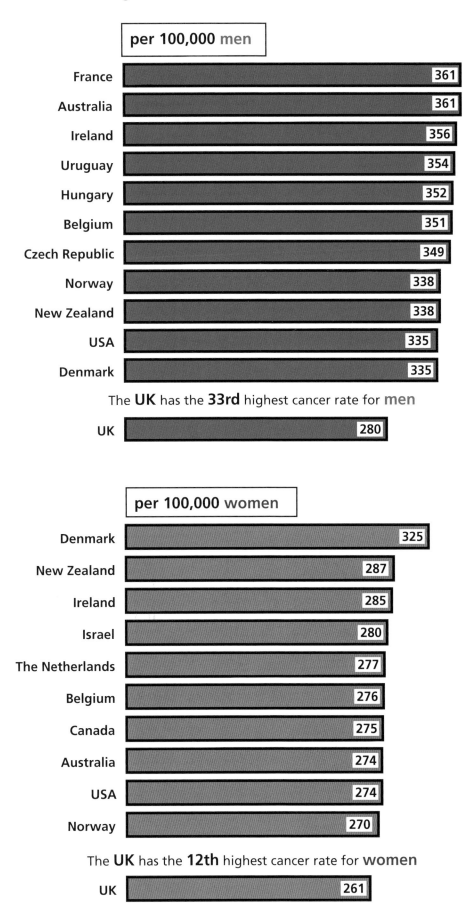

per 100,000 men

France	361
Australia	361
Ireland	356
Uruguay	354
Hungary	352
Belgium	351
Czech Republic	349
Norway	338
New Zealand	338
USA	335
Denmark	335

The **UK** has the **33rd** highest cancer rate for **men**

UK	280

per 100,000 women

Denmark	325
New Zealand	287
Ireland	285
Israel	280
The Netherlands	277
Belgium	276
Canada	275
Australia	274
USA	274
Norway	270

The **UK** has the **12th** highest cancer rate for **women**

UK	261

Source: World Cancer Research Fund
www.wcrf-uk.org

SEE ALSO:
Common cancers, p104
www.completeissues.co.uk

The big killers: TB

Worldwide, an estimated 1.7 million people died of TB and there were 9.4 million new cases, mainly in Asia and Africa

What is TB?

TB is an airborne disease – when people with TB cough, sneeze or spit, they propel the germs that cause TB into the air. A person can be infected by inhaling only a few of these germs.

TB can affect anyone and the bacteria can attack any part of the body, but most commonly the lungs.

It is more likely to affect people whose immune systems are already weakened such as people in poor countries – who may be malnourished and have poor access to healthcare generally and people with HIV.

People living with HIV are up to **50 times** more likely to develop TB than people free of HIV infection.

Without treatment, the vast majority of people living with HIV who are sick with TB will die within a few months.

400,000

Of the people who died of TB worldwide, **400,000** were infected with HIV. It is the leading cause of death among HIV infected people in Africa

---

TB can be cured with medication... but untreated it can kill

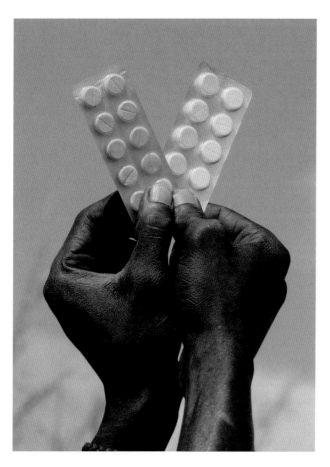

36 million

people have been cured of TB over the past 15 years. To ensure thorough treatment, it is often recommended that the patient takes his or her pills in the presence of someone who can supervise the therapy. This is called DOTS (directly observed treatment, short course).

Treatment usually takes six months with drugs that cost as little as **$10 per person** in some parts of the world.

8 million

TB deaths have been averted since the launch of DOTS in 1994, and the number of people being cured has increased regularly.

SEE ALSO:
TB in UK, p98
TB: 'I was a medical mystery',
p120, Essential Articles 14
www.completeissues.co.uk

The hardest hit countries

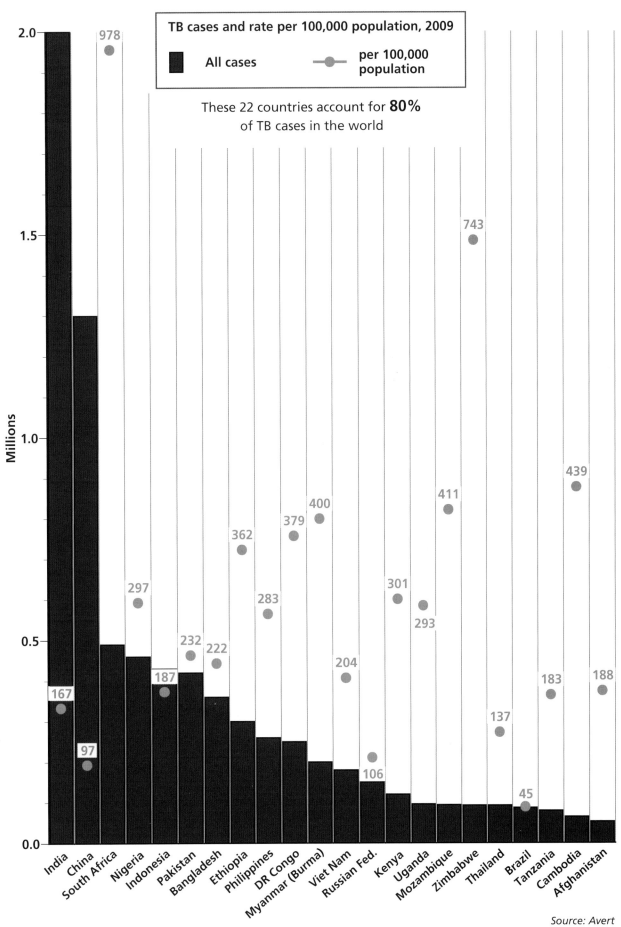

TB cases and rate per 100,000 population, 2009

■ All cases   ●— per 100,000 population

These 22 countries account for **80%** of TB cases in the world

Millions

2.0 — 978
1.5 — 743
1.0 — 439
      411
      400
      379
      362
      301
      297 293
0.5 — 283
      232 222
      204
      187
      167
      188
      183
      137
      106
      97
      45
0.0 —

India China South Africa Nigeria Indonesia Pakistan Bangladesh Ethiopia Philippines DR Congo Myanmar (Burma) Viet Nam Russian Fed. Kenya Uganda Mozambique Zimbabwe Thailand Brazil Tanzania Cambodia Afghanistan

Source: Avert
www.avert.org/tuberculosis.htm

Living with HIV

There are around 30.8 million adults and 2.5 million children living with HIV – but the world is beginning to reverse its spread

What is HIV?

HIV is a virus which can only grow or reproduce if it infects the cells of a living organism. HIV attacks the immune system itself – the very part of us that would normally get rid of a virus.

How is HIV treated?

Drugs can keep the levels of HIV in the body at a low level so the immune system has time to recover and work effectively. Treatment is limited in some parts of the world due to lack of funding.

How is HIV passed on?

- unprotected sex with an infected person;
- contact with an infected person's blood;
- use of infected blood products ie blood transfusions;
- sharing drug injection needles with an infected person;
- from mother to child – an estimated **370,000** children became infected with HIV in 2009. Most of these children are babies born to women with HIV. The child acquires the virus during pregnancy, labour or delivery, or through breast milk.

33.3 million

adults and children were estimated to be living with HIV in 2009, up slightly from 2008. This increase is mainly due to more people living longer as access to treatment becomes more widespread.

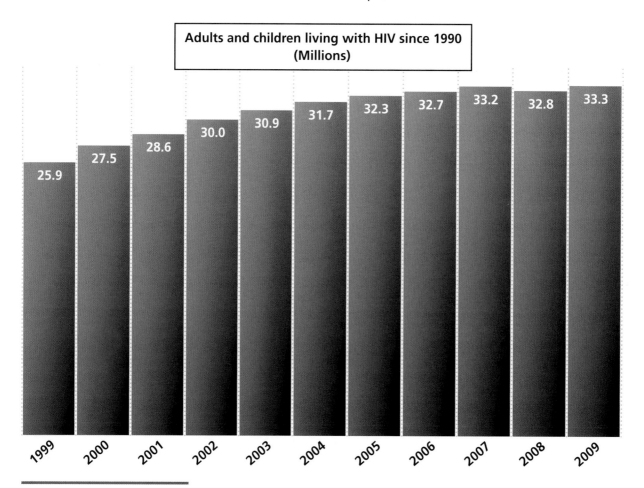

Adults and children living with HIV since 1990 (Millions)

1999	2000	2001	2002	2003	2004	2005	2006	2007	2008	2009
25.9	27.5	28.6	30.0	30.9	31.7	32.3	32.7	33.2	32.8	33.3

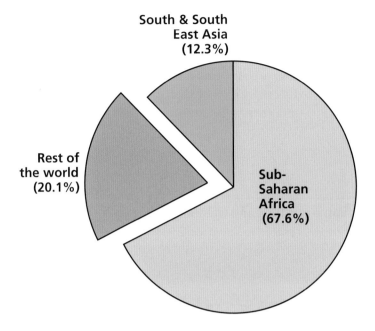

Where the 33.3 million adults and children with HIV live, by region, 2009

South & South East Asia (12.3%)

Rest of the world (20.1%)

Sub-Saharan Africa (67.6%)

Rest of the world breakdown	Proportion living with HIV
North America	4.5%
Eastern Europe & Central Asia	4.3%
Central & South America	4.2%
Western & Central Europe	2.5%
East Asia	2.3%
Middle East & North Africa	1.4%
Caribbean	0.7%
Oceania	0.2%

Rest of the world breakdown	Proportion newly infected
Eastern Europe & Central Asia	5.1%
Central & South America	3.6%
East Asia	3.2%
Middle East & North Africa	2.9%
North America	2.7%
Western & Central Europe	1.2%
Caribbean	0.7%
Oceania	0.2%

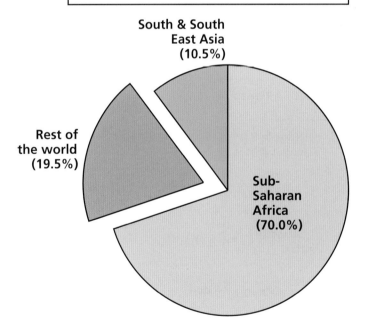

Where the 2.6 million newly infected people live, by region, 2009

South & South East Asia (10.5%)

Rest of the world (19.5%)

Sub-Saharan Africa (70.0%)

2.6 million

people became newly infected with HIV in 2009 – **20%** fewer than the **3.1 million** infected in 1999.

Among young people in 15 of the most severely affected countries, the rate of new HIV infections has fallen by **25%**, led by young people adopting safer sexual practices.

NB All figures are estimates, percentages may not add up to 100% due to rounding

Source: Avert; UNAIDS Report on the Global AIDS epidemic © 2010
www.avert.org/worldstatinfo.htm
www.unaids.org

SEE ALSO:
HIV UK, p96
www.completeissues.co.uk

Dying of AIDS

There are about 15 million people living with HIV in low- and middle-income countries who need treatment today

5.2 million

have access to treatment, so there are fewer AIDS-related deaths

However, **10 million** people living with HIV, who are eligible for treatment, are still in need.

How are HIV and AIDS connected?
HIV causes AIDS by damaging the immune system until it can no longer fight off other infections that it would usually be able to prevent.

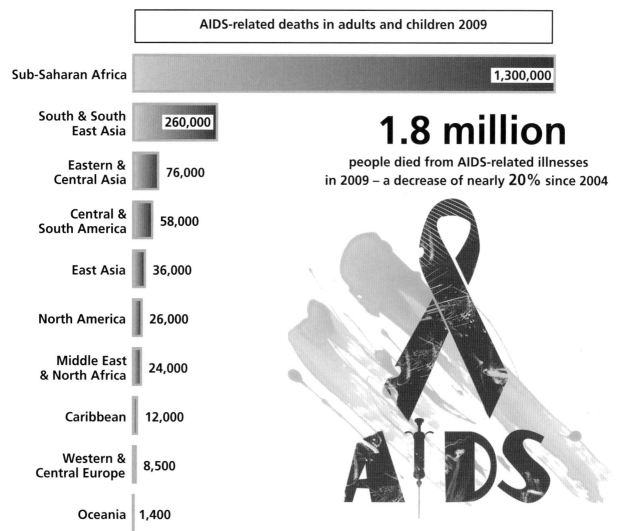

AIDS-related deaths in adults and children 2009

Region	Deaths
Sub-Saharan Africa	1,300,000
South & South East Asia	260,000
Eastern & Central Asia	76,000
Central & South America	58,000
East Asia	36,000
North America	26,000
Middle East & North Africa	24,000
Caribbean	12,000
Western & Central Europe	8,500
Oceania	1,400

1.8 million

people died from AIDS-related illnesses in 2009 – a decrease of nearly 20% since 2004

In 2009 alone, **1.2 million** people received HIV treatment for the first time – a **30%** increase compared to 2008.

Although the number of new HIV infections is decreasing, there are two new infections for every one person starting HIV treatment

A new approach – Treatment 2.0 – is being developed to improve the prevention and treatment of HIV on every level. This could prevent an additional **10 million** deaths by 2025 and reduce the number of people newly infected with HIV by up to **1 million** a year if countries provide treatment to all people in need.

Source: Avert; UNAIDS Report on the Global AIDS epidemic © 2010
www.avert.org/worldstatinfo.htm
www.unaids.org

SEE ALSO:
HIV UK, p96
www.completeissues.co.uk

Internet & media

GridNode
GridNode id="node 01"
Coordinate value="0.788297"
GridNodeBlock
Coordinate value="02"
Coordinate value="node 03"
Coordinate value="0.550734"
GridNodeBlock
Coordinate value="0.898938"
GridArray
DataStorage
DataStorage
Settings size_factor="1.07563" variation="9513" m
Intersection
Height value="1"
GridContext
Source value="SRC1024.16"
Propagation value="1"
Offset value="1"
Rotation value="0"
GridContext
Intersection
GridArray
Node id="node 01"
Coordinate value="0.895923"
NodeBlock
Node id="node 02"
ate id="node 03"
ate value="0.146101"
NodeBlock
value="0.561936"
ge
de
_factor="1.41047" variation="21608" map_type="0"
="1"
SRC1024.16"
lue="1"
"0"

3 01
C7"
02"

47" variation="10001" continuous="false" normali

169991

23.918237

16824.FG

15678236

Intersection
Height value
GridContext
Source value=""
Propagation value="1"
Offset value="0"
Rotation value="0"
GridContext
Intersection
GridArray
GridNode id="node 01"
GridNode id="0.788297"
GridNodeBlock
Coordinate value="node 02"
GridNode id="0.550734"
Coordinate value="node 03"
GridNode id="0.898938"
GridNodeBlock
GridArray
DataStorage
DataStorage
Settings size_factor="1.07563" variation="951
Intersection
Height value="1"
GridContext
Source value="SRC1024.16"
Propagation value="1"
Offset value="0"
Rotation value="0"
GridContext
Intersection
GridArray
GridNode id="node 01"
Coordinate va ue="0.895923"
Coordinate
Node Block
Node id= node
Coordinate value="0.146101"
GridNodeBlock
GridNode id="node 03"
Coordinate value="0.561936"
GridNodeBlock
GridArray
DataStorage
DataStorage
settings size_factor="1.41
Intersection
Height value="1"
GridContext
Source value="SRC1024.16"
Propagation value="1"
Offset value="1"
Rotation value="0"
GridContext
Intersection
618987
GridArray
GridNode id="node 01"
Coordinate value="0.97
GridNodeBlock
GridNode id="node 02"
Coordinate value="1"
GridNodeBlock
GridNode id="node 03"

Basic needs

One in three young people feel that internet access is as vital as air, food and water

When college students in 14 countries were asked about their attitudes to the internet **55%** agreed

"I could not live without the internet, it is an integral part of my daily life"

More questions revealed some surprising choices.

■	All
▨	UK

Do you consider the internet as important to your life as water, food, air, and shelter?

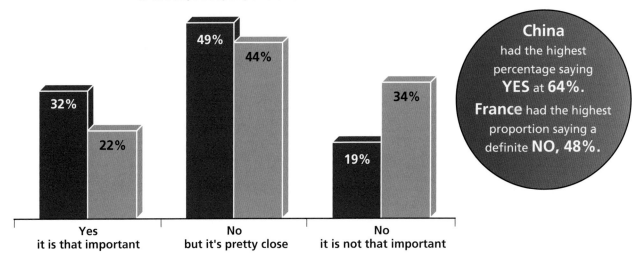

- Yes it is that important: **32%** (All), **22%** (UK)
- No but it's pretty close: **49%** (All), **44%** (UK)
- No it is not that important: **19%** (All), **34%** (UK)

China had the highest percentage saying **YES** at **64%**. **France** had the highest proportion saying a definite **NO, 48%.**

Which of the following is most important to you in your daily life?
(Select one)

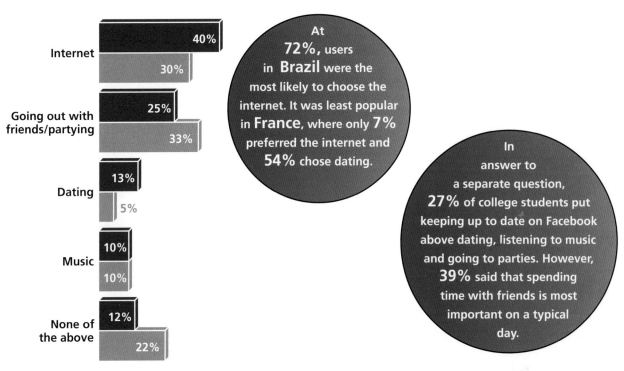

- Internet: **40%** (All), **30%** (UK)
- Going out with friends/partying: **25%** (All), **33%** (UK)
- Dating: **13%** (All), **5%** (UK)
- Music: **10%** (All), **10%** (UK)
- None of the above: **12%** (All), **22%** (UK)

At **72%**, users in **Brazil** were the most likely to choose the internet. It was least popular in **France**, where only **7%** preferred the internet and **54%** chose dating.

In answer to a separate question, **27%** of college students put keeping up to date on Facebook above dating, listening to music and going to parties. However, **39%** said that spending time with friends is most important on a typical day.

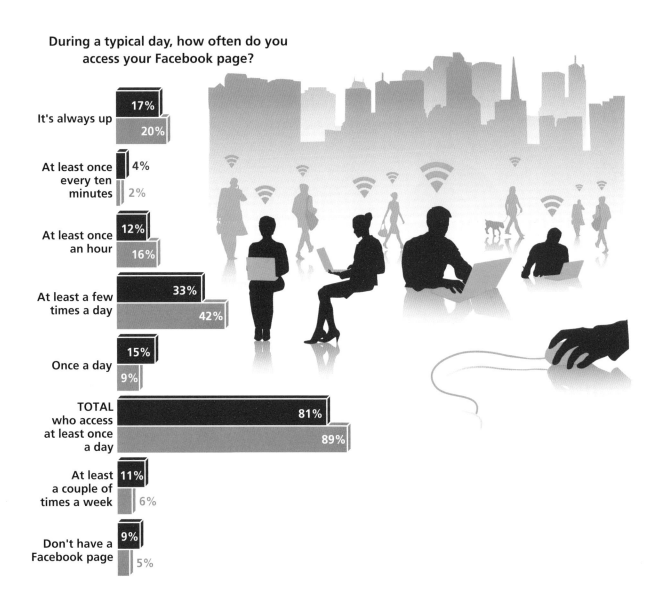

During a typical day, how often do you access your Facebook page?

- It's always up: 17% / 20%
- At least once every ten minutes: 4% / 2%
- At least once an hour: 12% / 16%
- At least a few times a day: 33% / 42%
- Once a day: 15% / 9%
- TOTAL who access at least once a day: 81% / 89%
- At least a couple of times a week: 11% / 6%
- Don't have a Facebook page: 9% / 5%

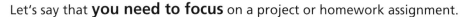

Let's say that **you need to focus** on a project or homework assignment.

In a typical hour, how many times are you distracted or interrupted by social media, IM, phone calls, a desire to check Facebook, etc?

(Select one)

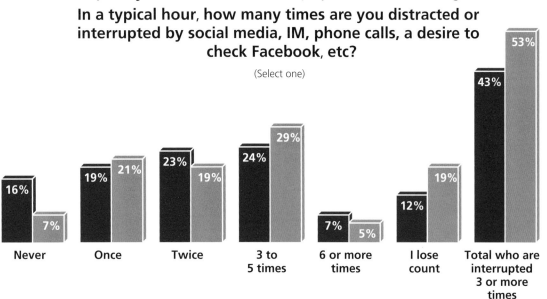

	Never	Once	Twice	3 to 5 times	6 or more times	I lose count	Total who are interrupted 3 or more times
	16% / 7%	19% / 21%	23% / 19%	24% / 29%	7% / 5%	12% / 19%	43% / 53%

Base: 1,441 College Students (age 18–24) in 14 countries, who completed an online survey between 13 May and 8 June, 2011
NB The fact that this was an online survey may have influenced results and the sample within each country will have been limited.

Source: The Cisco Connected World Technology Report, 2011
www.cisco.com/en

SEE ALSO:
Wasting time for fun, p134, Essential Articles
www.completeissues.co.uk

Generation app

People's relationships with their mobile phones have changed over recent years

There have been significant changes in the way people connect to the internet in recent years.

Almost half

of internet users used a mobile phone to connect to the internet, while away from the home or office in 2011.

There were

17.6 million

mobile phone internet users in 2011, representing **45%** of internet users, compared with **23%** in 2009.

An extra

6 million

people used their mobile phone to access the internet **for the first time** in the year between 2010 and 2011

Internet users who access via a mobile phone, GB

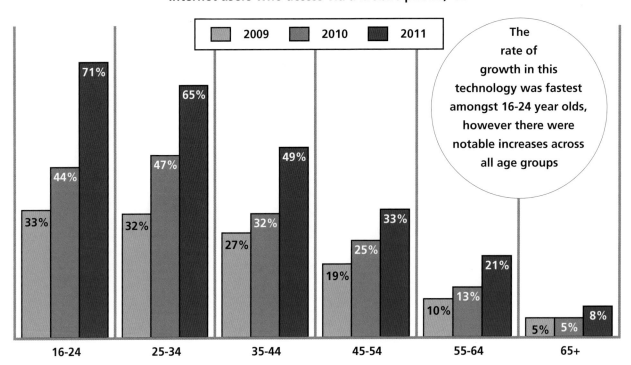

	2009	2010	2011
16-24	33%	44%	71%
25-34	32%	47%	65%
35-44	27%	32%	49%
45-54	19%	25%	33%
55-64	10%	13%	21%
65+	5%	5%	8%

The rate of growth in this technology was fastest amongst 16-24 year olds, however there were notable increases across all age groups

Source: Internet Access – Households and Individuals 2011,
Office for National Statistics © Crown copyright 2011
www.ons.gov.uk

Base 2,073 adults of which 26% were smartphone owners
NB Although official figures, note the low base

The rapid growth in the use of
Smartphones
is changing the way many of us, particularly teenagers, act in social situations

Compared to users of traditional mobile phones, smartphone users use their phone more and claim to be more addicted to their phone – **37%** of adults and **60%** of teens admit they are 'highly addicted'

27%
of adults and
47%
of teenagers
own a smartphone.

81%
of smartphone users make calls every day compared with
53%
of regular phone users.

79%
of smartphone owners claim to make and receive SMS texts on their mobile every day, compared to
50%
of regular phone users.

81%
of smartphone users have their mobile switched on all the time, even when they are in bed.

51%
of adults and
65%
of teenagers say they have used their smartphone while socialising with others.

47%
of adult Smartphone users have downloaded an app – many taking advantage of the free ones

Teens were more likely to use their smartphone in places where they've been asked to switch phones off ie the cinema or library –
27%
compared to
18%
of adults

23%
of adults and
34%
of teens have used them during mealtimes,
22%
of adults and
47%
of teens admitted using or answering their handset in the bathroom or toilet

38%
of teens had paid for an app compared to
25%
of adult owners
32%
of teens had paid for at least one game and
22%
had paid for a music based app

Source: Ofcom Communications Market Report, 2011
www.ofcom.org.uk

SEE ALSO:
www.completeissues.co.uk

Being sociable

Users are most likely to use social networks for interacting and keeping up to date with friends...

Respondents were asked:
What are the benefits to you of using social networks?
Base: All who use social networks 1,685

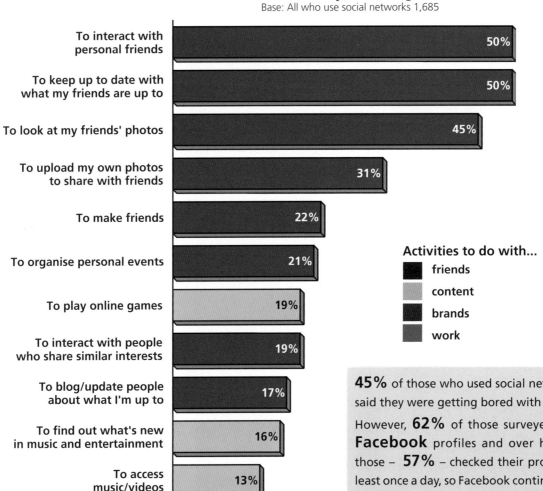

To interact with personal friends	50%
To keep up to date with what my friends are up to	50%
To look at my friends' photos	45%
To upload my own photos to share with friends	31%
To make friends	22%
To organise personal events	21%
To play online games	19%
To interact with people who share similar interests	19%
To blog/update people about what I'm up to	17%
To find out what's new in music and entertainment	16%
To access music/videos	13%
To keep up to date with my favourite brands	13%
To stay in touch with special offers from brands	13%
To receive promotional benefits/ vouchers from companies	11%
To promote myself/ my website	10%
To belong to a professional network	9%
For work purposes	8%
Other	2%
None of these	13%

Activities to do with...
- friends
- content
- brands
- work

45% of those who used social networks said they were getting bored with them.

However, **62%** of those surveyed had **Facebook** profiles and over half of those – **57%** – checked their profile at least once a day, so Facebook continues to dominate as the main platform for social network activity.

Source: 2011 Digital Entertainment Survey
from Entertainment Media Research
www.wiggin.co.uk

...and the average Facebook user has 130 friends

Facebook users worldwide

| ■ | Millions of Facebook users as at 30/6/11 | ✓ | Penetration (% of Facebook users in relation to the total estimated population in each region) |

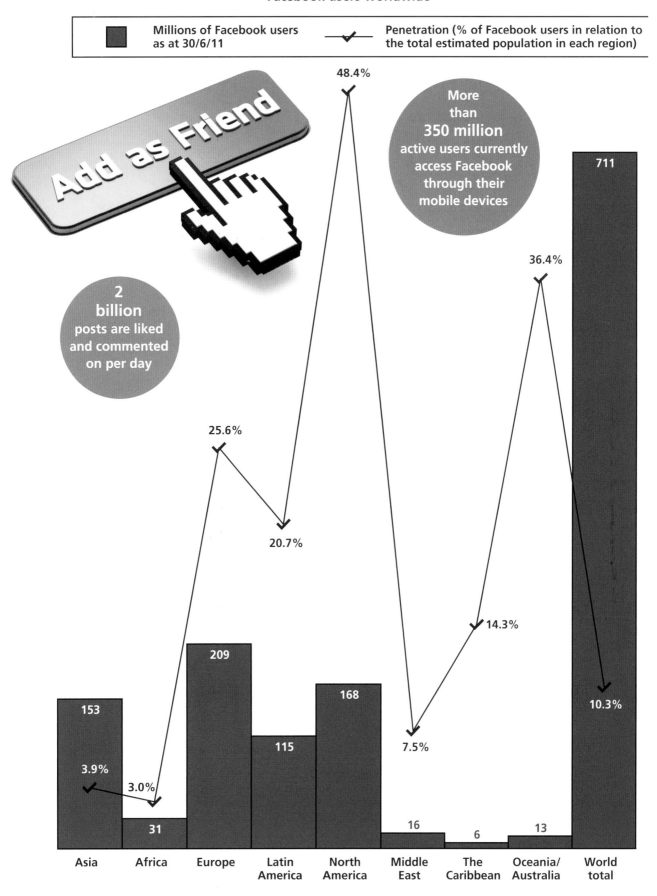

Add as Friend

More than 350 million active users currently access Facebook through their mobile devices

2 billion posts are liked and commented on per day

48.4%
36.4%
25.6%
20.7%
14.3%
7.5%
10.3%
3.9%
3.0%

711

209
168
153
115
31
16
6
13

Asia | Africa | Europe | Latin America | North America | Middle East | The Caribbean | Oceania/ Australia | World total

Source: Internet World Stats; Facebook statistics
www.internetworldstats.com/facebook.htm
www.facebook.com

SEE ALSO:
Wasting time for fun, p134, Essential Articles
www.completeissues.co.uk

Who's online?

Internet users in Europe

There were **2.1 billion internet** users in the world in 2011 – **476 million** were in Europe.

58.3% of the European population were internet users, the world average was **30.5%**

Top 10 internet countries in Europe and % penetration

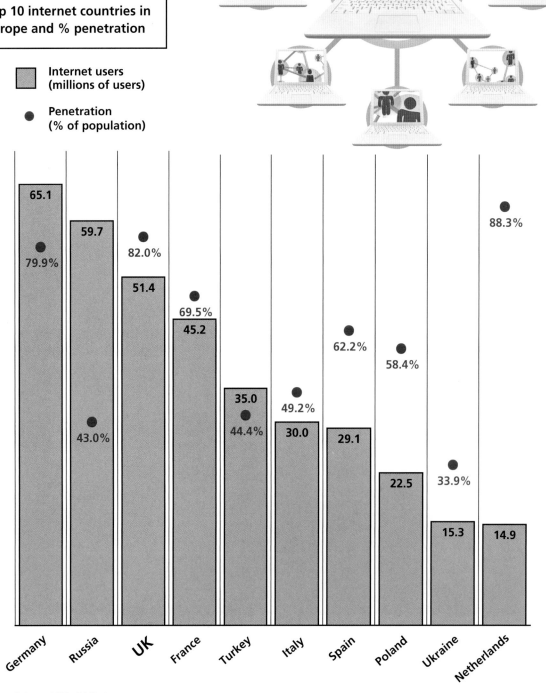

- Internet users (millions of users)
- ● Penetration (% of population)

Country	Internet users (millions)	Penetration
Germany	65.1	79.9%
Russia	59.7	43.0%
UK	51.4	82.0%
France	45.2	69.5%
Turkey	35.0	44.4%
Italy	30.0	49.2%
Spain	29.1	62.2%
Poland	22.5	58.4%
Ukraine	15.3	33.9%
Netherlands	14.9	88.3%

Source: Internet World Stats
www.internetworldstats.com

SEE ALSO:
www.completeissues.co.uk

Law & order

I predict a riot

Who was in court after the August 2011 riots... and what happened to them?

6th August, 2011: A peaceful march against a police shooting in Tottenham, London, was followed by a riot. Over the following days rioting spread to other areas of London and to other cities.

The purpose of the original demonstration was lost in the widespread looting and arson attacks which followed. The disorder led to five deaths and many injuries – but there was also a response from the wider community in the form of clean up campaigns and donations to victims.

More than 3,000 arrests were made.
1,984 people had appeared before the courts by 12th October 2011 –
90% were male and **10%** were female.

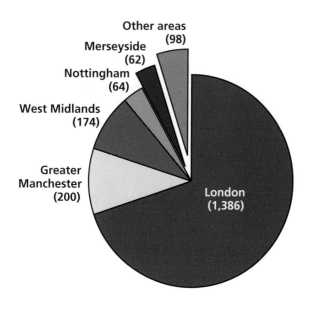

Cases by area – first hearings

Other areas (98)
Merseyside (62)
Nottingham (64)
West Midlands (174)
Greater Manchester (200)
London (1,386)

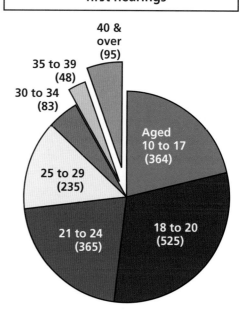

Ages and number of those in court – first hearings

40 & over (95)
35 to 39 (48)
30 to 34 (83)
25 to 29 (235)
Aged 10 to 17 (364)
21 to 24 (365)
18 to 20 (525)

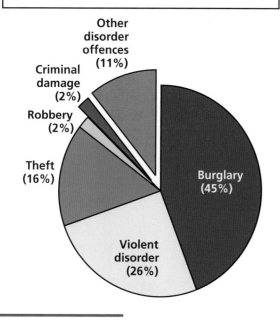

What offences the first hearings were for

Other disorder offences (11%)
Criminal damage (2%)
Robbery (2%)
Theft (16%)
Burglary (45%)
Violent disorder (26%)

Are the sentences tougher?

551 of the **1,984** people brought before the courts had been found guilty and sentenced for their part in the disorder by 12/10/11.

331 were given immediate prison sentences with an average length of **12.5 months**. This compares to **3.7 months** for those convicted for similar offences in 2010.

NB Figures may not add up to 100% due to rounding

36% of young people had been suspended from school at least once in a year compared to **6%** of all Year 11 pupils

3% had been excluded from school compared to **0.1%** of all Year 11 pupils

Characteristics of those appearing in court compared to national average

71% of males aged 18-52 had at least one previous **conviction** compared to **28%** of the population as a whole

80% of adults who appeared before the courts for the disorder had a previous **caution or conviction**

45% of males aged 10-17 had at least one previous **conviction** compared to **2%** of the population as a whole

62% of juveniles who had appeared before the courts for the disorder had a previous **caution or conviction**

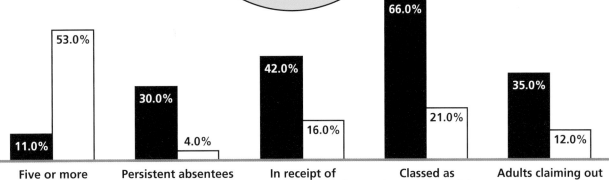

■ Riot suspects

□ National average

	Five or more A* to C grades at GCSE (inc. English & Maths)	Persistent absentees from school	In receipt of Free School Meals (secondary schools)	Classed as having a Special Educational Need	Adults claiming out of work benefit
Riot suspects	11.0%	30.0%	42.0%	66.0%	35.0%
National average	53.0%	4.0%	16.0%	21.0%	12.0%

A NatCen study of young people involved in the disorder concluded that they were driven by a combination of the party atmosphere, adrenaline, hype, the thrill of getting free stuff and dissatisfaction with the police
www.natcen.ac.uk/study/the-august-riots-in-england-

Source: Statistical bulletin on the public disorder of 6th to 9th August 2011, Ministry of Justice © Crown copyright 2011
www.justice.gov.uk

SEE ALSO:
www.completeissues.co.uk

Locked up

More than 10.1 million people are held in prisons throughout the world

Ten highest world prison population rates, per 100,000 of national population

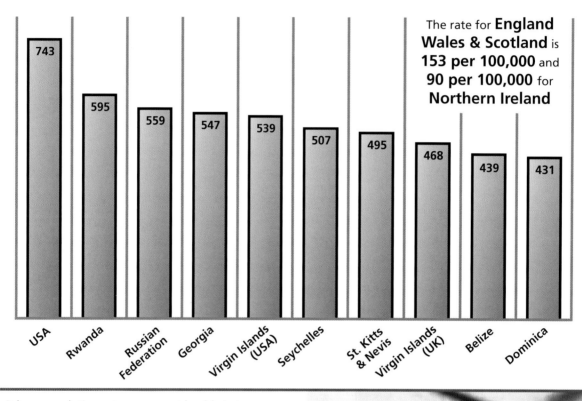

The rate for **England Wales & Scotland** is **153 per 100,000** and **90 per 100,000** for **Northern Ireland**

USA	743
Rwanda	595
Russian Federation	559
Georgia	547
Virgin Islands (USA)	539
Seychelles	507
St. Kitts & Nevis	495
Virgin Islands (UK)	468
Belize	439
Dominica	431

Prison population rates vary considerably between different regions of the world, and even between different parts of the same continent eg:

- in western Africa the rate is **47.5 per 100,000** compared to **219 per 100,000** in southern Africa

- in South American countries the rate is **175 per 100,000** compared to **357.5 per 100,000** in Caribbean countries

- in south central Asian countries (mainly the Indian sub-continent) the rate is **42 per 100,000** compared to **155.5 per 100,000** for eastern Asian countries

- in western European countries the rate is **96 per 100,000** compared to **228 per 100,000** in countries spanning Europe and Asia (eg Russia and Turkey)

- in Oceania (including Australia and New Zealand) the rate is **135 per 100,000**

Prison populations are growing everywhere and have risen in **78%** of countries.

NB Median rates are used throughout because different countries have different practices and figures relate to most recent dates available, not to the same years

Almost half of sentenced prisoners are in three countries:
United States – 2.29m, Russia – 0.81m and **China – 1.65m**.
There are more than **650,000** people in 'detention centres' in China – making the overall Chinese total **over 2.3m** and the world total more than **10.75m**.

There is no agreement about how much space or what facilities prisoners should have.

The percentages in the table show the *occupancy rate* – whether a prison system holds more prisoners than it is intended to hold and, if so, by how much.

This is not the same thing as the level of overcrowding, but it may be the best measure of overcrowding that is available.

Occupancy rate in the 16 countries with the highest percentage of people in prison awaiting trial (pre-trial detainees)

Country	Pre-trial detainees (% of prison population)	Occupancy rate
Mali	88.7%	223.3%
Liberia	around 85%	136.3%
Togo	around 80%	not available
Bolivia	78.7%	185.1%
Niger	around 76%	64.6%
Benin	74.9%	307.1%
Paraguay	71.2%	105.5%
Pakistan	70.7%	177.4%
Congo (Brazzaville)	around 70%	not available
Nigeria	69.2%	84.1%
Bangladesh	69.0%	238.2%
Haiti	67.6%	335.7%
Republic of Guinea	67.2%	174.8%
India	67.0%	129.2%
Venezuela	66.2%	117.4%
Uruguay	65.2%	128.4%

Of these 16 countries, **10** have high rates of occupancy classed as **over 120%**.

Haiti

The most recent figures available show that Haiti has the highest level of over-occupation:

Official capacity of prison system: **2,448**

Prison population total (including pre-trial detainees/remand prisoners): **5,331**

Prison population rate (per 100,000 of national population): **55**

Source: International Centre for Prison Studies, World Prison Population List 9th edition, World Prison Brief May 2011 & Current Situation of Prison Overcrowding 2010
www.prisonstudies.org

SEE ALSO:
Prison population, p126
www.completeissues.co.uk

Who's inside?

Characteristics of the prison population in England and Wales

47% of male sentenced prisoners and

50% of female sentenced prisoners had run away from home as a child – this compares to **10%** of the general population

Only **2%** of the general population had been taken into care as a child. For prisoners the figure is **25%**

20% of women prisoners were living at home with dependent children at the time of imprisonment.

43% of prisoners had a family member who had been convicted of a criminal offence

35% had a family member who had been in prison

25% of young male offenders in prison are fathers.

81% of prisoners were unmarried prior to imprisonment, rising to **85%** since imprisonment.

Almost **10%** had been divorced. These figures are **twice** as high as those found in the general population

50%

of male and

33%

of female sentenced prisoners had been excluded from school.

You need reading, writing and number skills at the level of at least an 11 year old to manage everyday tasks.

66%

of prisoners have **number** skills at or below this level

50%

have a **reading** ability at or below this level and

82%

have a **writing** ability at or below this level.

50%

of male and

70%

of female prisoners have no qualifications.

5% of men and 2% of women in the general population suffer from two or more mental disorders. For prisoners the figure is around

70%

66%

of prisoners were unemployed in the four weeks before they went to prison.

Nearly

75%

of prisoners were in receipt of benefits immediately before entering prison.

5%

of prisoners were sleeping rough and almost

33%

were not living in permanent accommodation immediately before they went to prison

Prisoners are more likely to be abusers of illegal drugs and alcohol than other sectors of the community.

Source: House of Commons May 2011
www.parliament.uk/topics/Prisons.htm

SEE ALSO:
A radical alternative to prison? p154, Essential Articles 13
www.completeissues.co.uk

Prison population

Make up of the prison population in England and Wales

The prison population in England and Wales has been increasing steadily over the past hundred years.

In 2008 the prison population was bigger than the number that the prisons could officially hold for the first time in history.

From 1990-2010, the number of female prisoners increased by **almost a third**, a slightly higher rate of increase than for male prisoners.

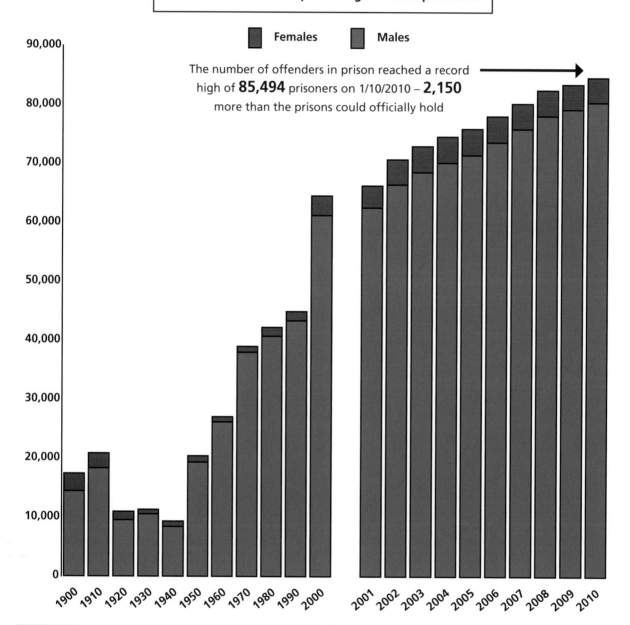

Average prison population 1900-2010, England and Wales and females as percentage of total prisoners

Females   Males

The number of offenders in prison reached a record high of **85,494** prisoners on 1/10/2010 – **2,150** more than the prisons could officially hold

STOP PRESS: 4th November 2011

Prison numbers reached a record high of **87,749** (including those being held on remand) due to the August 2011 riots. The riots will see prisons swell by up to 1,000 extra inmates over 2012 and the effects will continue until August 2013.

Source: Ministry of Justice © Crown copyright
www.justice.gov.uk

SEE ALSO:
I predict a riot, p120
Locked up, p122
A radical alternative to prison?
p154, Essential Articles 13
www.completeissues.co.uk

Population

Population clock

The global population rose to 6.9 billion in 2010, with nearly all of that growth in the world's developing countries

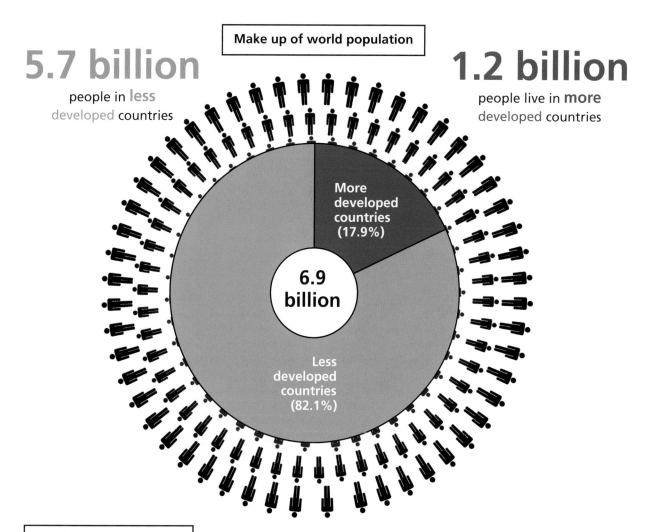

Make up of world population

5.7 billion
people in **less**
developed countries

1.2 billion
people live in **more**
developed countries

More
developed
countries
(17.9%)

6.9
billion

Less
developed
countries
(82.1%)

Births
per year

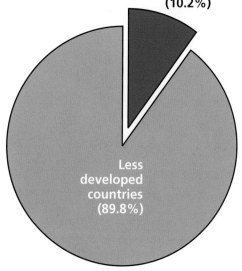

More
developed
countries
(10.2%)

Less
developed
countries
(89.8%)

140,213,443
yearly births worldwide
equivalent to **384,146** per day or
267 per minute

Births per	More developed countries	Less developed countries
Year	14,245,797	125,967,646
Day	39,030	345,117
Minute	27	240

NB Figures may not add up due to rounding

Deaths
per year

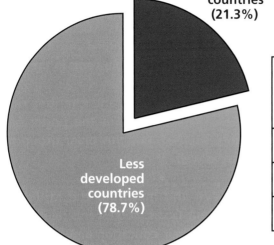

More developed countries (21.3%)

Less developed countries (78.7%)

56,897,968
yearly deaths worldwide
equivalent to **155,885** per day or
108 per minute

Deaths per	More developed countries	Less developed countries
Year	12,115,417	44,782,552
Day	33,193	122,692
Minute	23	85

Natural Increase
(births minus deaths per year)

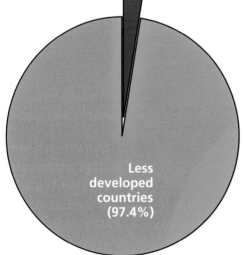

More developed countries (2.6%)

Less developed countries (97.4%)

83,315,475
yearly increase in population worldwide
equivalent to **228,262** per day or
159 per minute

"There are two major trends in world population today. On the one hand, chronically low birth rates in **developed countries** are beginning to challenge the health and financial security of their elderly. On the other, the **developing countries** are adding over **80 million** to the population every year and the poorest of those countries are adding **20 million**, exacerbating poverty and threatening the environment."

Bill Butz, President, Population Reference Bureau

Natural increase per	More developed countries	Less developed countries
Year	2,130,380	81,185,094
Day	5,837	222,425
Minute	4	154

The population is increasing because the death rate has gone down and the birth rate has not slowed as much as expected

Source: Population Reference Bureau
www.prb.org

SEE ALSO:
www.completeissues.co.uk

Future generation

Young people make up 18% of the world's population

The number of adolescents – young people aged 10-19 – has more than doubled since 1950. There are now **1.2 billion** adolescents in the world.

Development agencies and charities rightly emphasise investment in the under 5s, to promote survival, but this older group need support as well.

To achieve and maintain the Millennium Development Goals, adolescents need support to continue their education and be protected from early marriage, childbearing etc. to allow them to fulfil their potential.

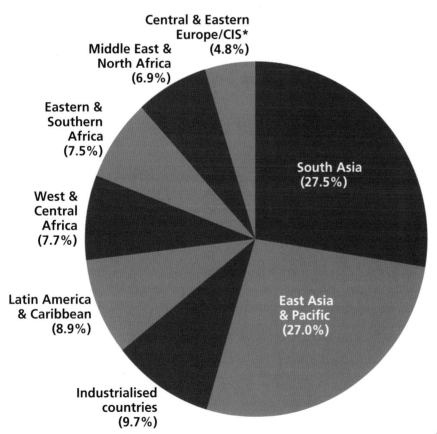

Adolescent population by region, 2009

- Central & Eastern Europe/CIS* (4.8%)
- Middle East & North Africa (6.9%)
- Eastern & Southern Africa (7.5%)
- West & Central Africa (7.7%)
- Latin America & Caribbean (8.9%)
- Industrialised countries (9.7%)
- South Asia (27.5%)
- East Asia & Pacific (27.0%)

88%
of adolescents live in developing countries

More than half the world's adolescents live in either South Asia or the East Asia and Pacific region –around **330 million** in each

In 2050 sub-Saharan Africa is projected to have more adolescents than any other region

*Commonwealth of Independent States (former Soviet Union)

Highest adolescent population

The highest proportion of adolescents, 26%,
live in Zimbabwe, Samoa and Swaziland

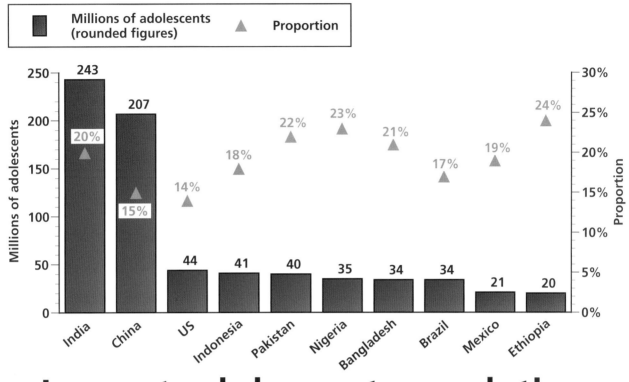

Lowest adolescent population

The lowest proportion of adolescents, 9%,
live in Spain, Italy and Japan

12%
of the UK
population
is adolescent

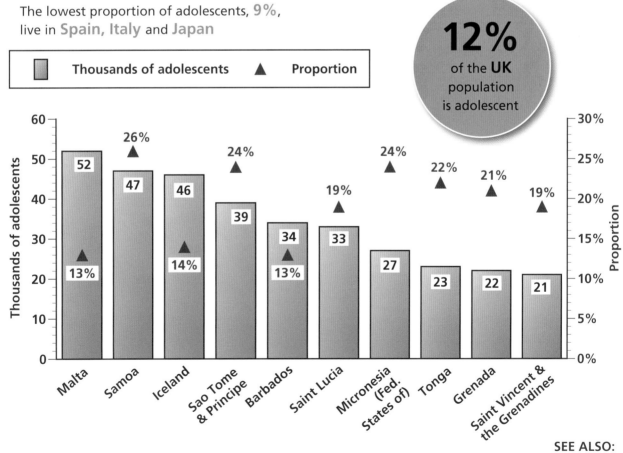

Source: State of the World's Children 2011
www.unicef.org/sowc2011

SEE ALSO:
Age concern, p168, Fact File 2010

www.completeissues.co.uk

Shape of things to come?

The population of developed countries is ageing and there is little growth. In developing countries the population is young and is growing

More developed countries 2012

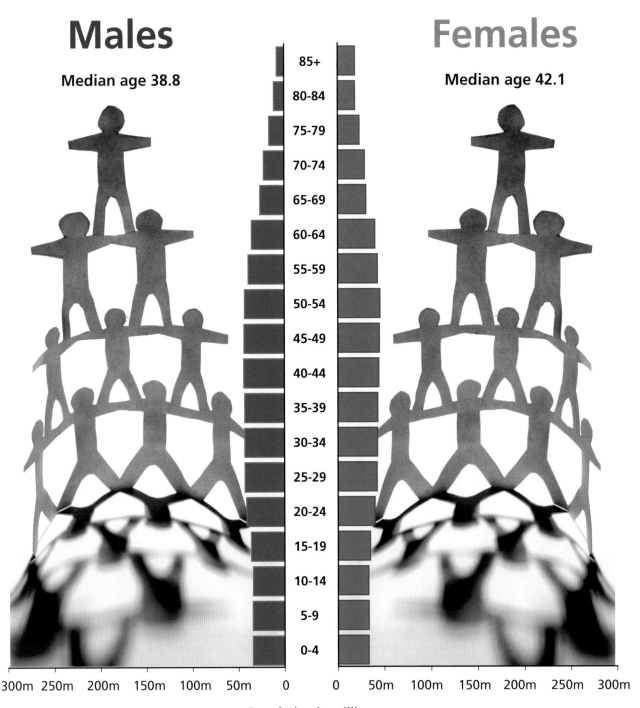

Males
Median age 38.8

Females
Median age 42.1

| 85+ |
| 80-84 |
| 75-79 |
| 70-74 |
| 65-69 |
| 60-64 |
| 55-59 |
| 50-54 |
| 45-49 |
| 40-44 |
| 35-39 |
| 30-34 |
| 25-29 |
| 20-24 |
| 15-19 |
| 10-14 |
| 5-9 |
| 0-4 |

300m 250m 200m 150m 100m 50m 0   0 50m 100m 150m 200m 250m 300m

Population in millions

The population 'pyramid' of the developed countries clearly shows the decline in the number of young people as a result of low birth rates.

In some developed countries the size of the youngest age group is barely more than half that of their parents' age group.

When the two population pyramids are compared, it is obvious that virtually all future world population growth will take place in the developing countries.

But the amount of growth these countries will experience depends upon the degree to which couples in those countries choose to reduce family size and have access to family planning services.

Less developed countries 2012

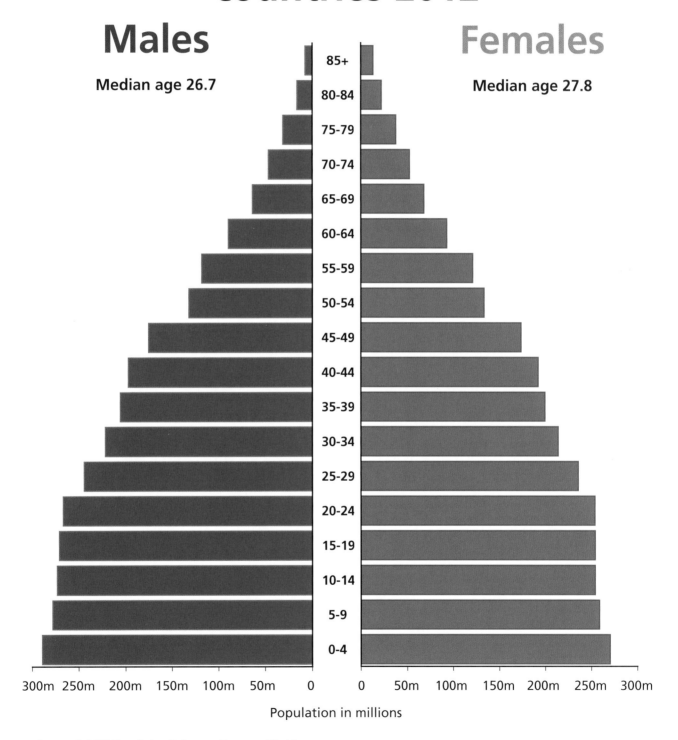

Males

Median age 26.7

Females

Median age 27.8

Population in millions

Source: © 2010 Population Reference Bureau – World Population Data Sheet; US Census International Database
www.prb.org
www.census.gov/ipc/www/idb/index.php

SEE ALSO:
www.completeissues.co.uk

Full stop?

World population has reached 7 billion. Will it continue to increase or will we see 'zero population growth'?

World population has reached a changing point: the huge growth of the second half of the 20th century has slowed. But factors such as better life expectancy and slower-than-expected declines in birth rates will mean growth for decades. The questions remain: **how fast, how much and where?**

DEVELOPED COUNTRIES:

The **POPULATION** size of the world's more developed countries has **PEAKED**. Birth rates have declined and life expectancy has improved.

Because of this many more developed countries may decline in size and see the proportion of their **ELDERLY POPULATIONS** rise to new levels.

Any growth will mostly come from immigration from less developed countries.

LESS DEVELOPED COUNTRIES:

The world population increased from 1.6 billion in 1900 to 6.1 billion in 2000. This population growth was almost entirely due to the rapid **DECLINE IN DEATH RATES** in less developed countries.

As a result, many adopted policies to **LOWER THE BIRTH RATE**. This made a bigger impact in some countries than others.

The total fertility rate (TFR) in less developed countries declined from 6.0 in the early 1950s to 2.5 today.

TFR is the average number of children born to a woman over her lifetime.

WORLD POPULATION

Projections of world population in 2050 currently range from 9.15 billion to 9.51 billion. These projections have assumed that the TFR will decline to two children or less in developing countries. This depends on women's desire to use family planning. The ability to do so, in turn, depends on governments providing family planning services. Decline in TFR is slowing in some countries and has barely begun in others.

Sport &
leisure

'To do' list

Heritage, sport and shopping are top attractions for visitors to Britain

Researchers interviewed approximately 10,000 adults in 20 nations around the world and asked them to pick the things they'd like to do most whilst visiting Britain.

Which of the following activities would tourists most like to do while visiting Britain?

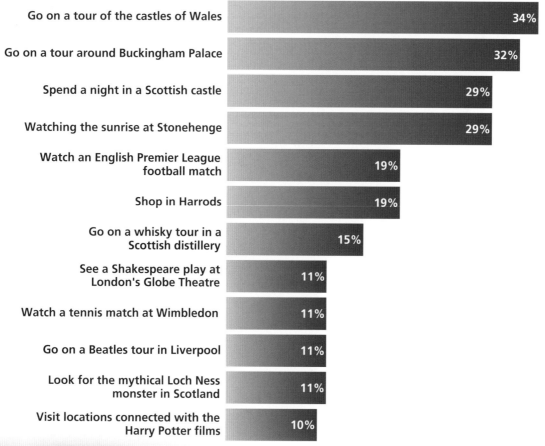

Activity	%
Go on a tour of the castles of Wales	34%
Go on a tour around Buckingham Palace	32%
Spend a night in a Scottish castle	29%
Watching the sunrise at Stonehenge	29%
Watch an English Premier League football match	19%
Shop in Harrods	19%
Go on a whisky tour in a Scottish distillery	15%
See a Shakespeare play at London's Globe Theatre	11%
Watch a tennis match at Wimbledon	11%
Go on a Beatles tour in Liverpool	11%
Look for the mythical Loch Ness monster in Scotland	11%
Visit locations connected with the Harry Potter films	10%

There was an interesting difference in what people wanted to do,
between different types of people from different nations

The Gender gap

27% of men and 8% of women wanted to see a Premier League match, while 24% of women and 14% of men wanted to shop at Harrods. 38% of women and 31% of men would tour castles in Wales, 36% of women and 29% of men would visit Buckingham Palace and 31% of women and 28% of men would like to spend the night in a Scottish Castle.

The Generation gap

The appeal of the Scottish whisky distilleries increased with age, chosen by 12% of 18-24s but 22% of over 65s. But the 18-24s were more likely than over 65s to choose to see an English Premier League football match (22% versus 9%), and visiting locations associated with the Harry Potter films (15% versus 2%).

Going on a Beatles tour in Liverpool had most appeal for those aged 45-54, 15%, and those aged 55-64, 16%, than other ages.

The nation division

18% of South Koreans wanted to visit locations connected to the Harry Potter films. Touring the castles of Wales was popular in almost all countries – Poland 49%, Russia 48%, Italy 46% and Germany 44% scored these highest. 54% of Russians were keenest to tour Buckingham Palace. Swedes were particularly keen on spending a night in a Scottish castle, 40%, as were Italians 39%, Americans 35%, Mexicans 34%, French 34% and Canadians 33%.

Sporting nations

Watching an English Premier League game most appealed to visitors from Egypt – 32%, Turkey – 30%, South Africa – 31%, India – 24%, China – 24%, Argentina – 22%, Brazil – 20%, Mexico – 20%, Sweden – 22% and Poland – 22%.

Caerphilly Castle

SEE ALSO:
Travel trends, p152

Source: VisitBritain
www.visitbritain.com

www.completeissues.co.uk

Running out of time?

Although 53% of women want to do more sport, far fewer women than men are getting sporty

3 x 30 is the minimum recommended amount of exercise needed to maintain basic good health.

Percentage of men and women who participated in 3 x 30 minutes of sport per week.

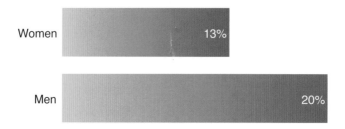

Women — 13%

Men — 20%

Between 2008-09 and 2009-10 there was a slight increase in the number of women participating regularly in sport - up 35,000 to 2.76 million (12.8%). There are still over 1.4 million more men taking part in sport.

The greatest difference between men and women is at age 19 when double the proportion of men than women do sport regularly.

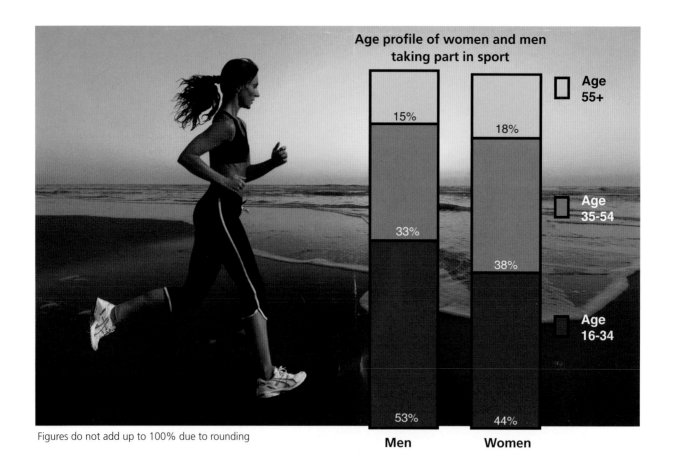

Age profile of women and men taking part in sport

Men: 15%, 33%, 53%
Women: 18%, 38%, 44%

Age 55+
Age 35-54
Age 16-34

Figures do not add up to 100% due to rounding

Proportion of women and men who take part in sport by whether they have children in the household

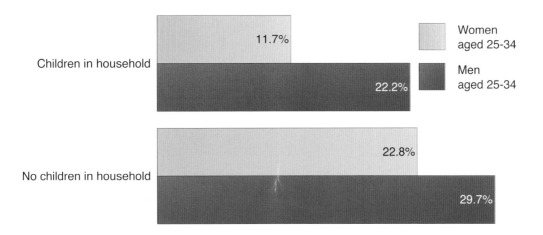

Children in household

11.7%

22.2%

No children in household

22.8%

29.7%

Women aged 25-34

Men aged 25-34

Barriers to sport

- Ageing – participation declines as women get older and other commitments prevent involvement, this is also similar for men.

- Income – women from low income households have the lowest levels of involvement.

- Physiological and cultural barriers – such as body consciousness and experiences at school that have a negative influence on women.

Percentage of women who want to do more sport than they do now

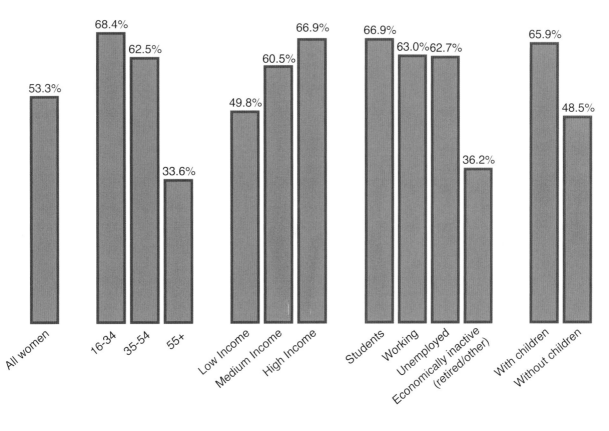

All women	16-34	35-54	55+	Low Income	Medium Income	High Income	Students	Working	Unemployed	Economically inactive (retired/other)	With children	Without children
53.3%	68.4%	62.5%	33.6%	49.8%	60.5%	66.9%	66.9%	63.0%	62.7%	36.2%	65.9%	48.5%

Source: Women's participation in sport,
Women's Sport and Fitness Foundation
wsff.org.uk

SEE ALSO:
www.completeissues.co.uk

Support for sport

Attitudes towards the 2012 Olympic Games

How do you feel about the UK hosting the 2012 Olympic Games?

Base: 14,102 adults aged 16+ in England

Slightly or strongly against (10.2%)

Neither against nor supportive (23.0%)

Slightly or strongly supportive (66.4%)

Reasons for being strongly supportive of the UK hosting the Olympics

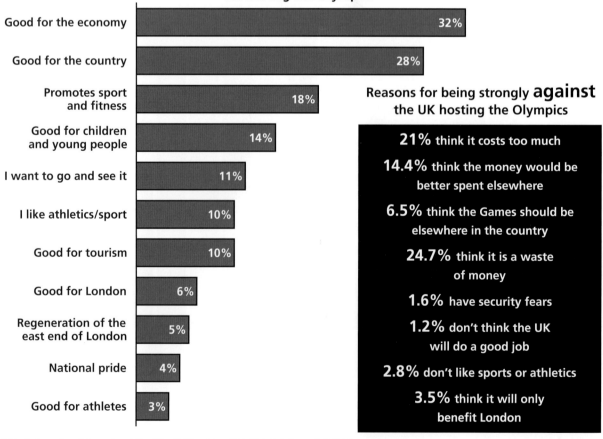

Good for the economy	32%
Good for the country	28%
Promotes sport and fitness	18%
Good for children and young people	14%
I want to go and see it	11%
I like athletics/sport	10%
Good for tourism	10%
Good for London	6%
Regeneration of the east end of London	5%
National pride	4%
Good for athletes	3%

Reasons for being strongly against the UK hosting the Olympics

21% think it costs too much

14.4% think the money would be better spent elsewhere

6.5% think the Games should be elsewhere in the country

24.7% think it is a waste of money

1.6% have security fears

1.2% don't think the UK will do a good job

2.8% don't like sports or athletics

3.5% think it will only benefit London

This Cultural and Sporting Life: The Taking Part 2010/11 Adult and Child Report, August 2011, Department for culture media & sport © Crown copyright 2011 www.culture.gov.uk

SEE ALSO:
www.completeissues.co.uk

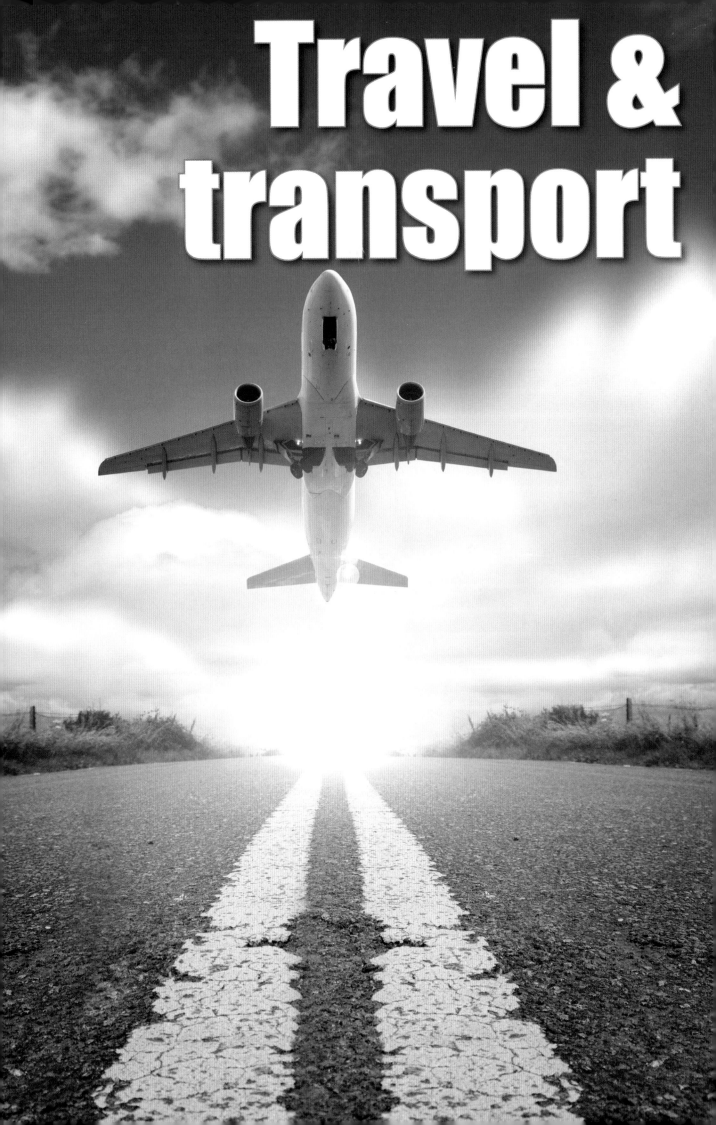

Travel & transport

Falling fatalities

Over the course of a decade, road deaths have reduced dramatically in high income countries. But 90% of road deaths in the world occur in low and middle income countries

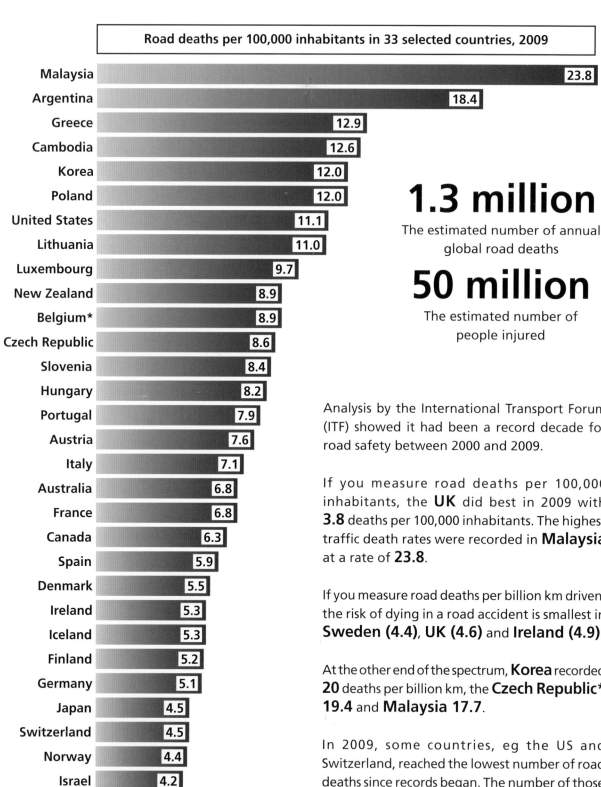

Road deaths per 100,000 inhabitants in 33 selected countries, 2009

Malaysia	23.8
Argentina	18.4
Greece	12.9
Cambodia	12.6
Korea	12.0
Poland	12.0
United States	11.1
Lithuania	11.0
Luxembourg	9.7
New Zealand	8.9
Belgium*	8.9
Czech Republic	8.6
Slovenia	8.4
Hungary	8.2
Portugal	7.9
Austria	7.6
Italy	7.1
Australia	6.8
France	6.8
Canada	6.3
Spain	5.9
Denmark	5.5
Ireland	5.3
Iceland	5.3
Finland	5.2
Germany	5.1
Japan	4.5
Switzerland	4.5
Norway	4.4
Israel	4.2
Netherlands	3.9
Sweden	3.9
UK	3.8

* 2008

1.3 million
The estimated number of annual global road deaths

50 million
The estimated number of people injured

Analysis by the International Transport Forum (ITF) showed it had been a record decade for road safety between 2000 and 2009.

If you measure road deaths per 100,000 inhabitants, the **UK** did best in 2009 with **3.8** deaths per 100,000 inhabitants. The highest traffic death rates were recorded in **Malaysia** at a rate of **23.8**.

If you measure road deaths per billion km driven, the risk of dying in a road accident is smallest in **Sweden (4.4)**, **UK (4.6)** and **Ireland (4.9)**.

At the other end of the spectrum, **Korea** recorded **20** deaths per billion km, the **Czech Republic*** **19.4** and **Malaysia 17.7**.

In 2009, some countries, eg the US and Switzerland, reached the lowest number of road deaths since records began. The number of those killed and injured in Denmark was at its lowest level since 1932 and the improved level of road safety in Canada resulted in their lowest death toll in more than 60 years.

Three of the 33 countries analysed by the ITF's International Traffic Safety Data and Analysis Group (IRTAD Group) showed an increase in road deaths over the 2000-2009 period.

Both **Argentina and Malaysia** showed increases of **12%** and **Cambodia** increased by **328%. Cambodia's** huge deterioration in road safety is due to a variety of factors:

- the large increase in number of vehicles
- the growing population of young people (who are the most at risk) and their lack of safety education; and, surprisingly
- improvement of their roads – this has allowed higher speeds which is particularly dangerous when a variety of users, including vulnerable road users, share the same road space

Argentina, Malaysia and Cambodia have only recently joined the IRTAD Group and hope to benefit from road safety measures in the future.

Traffic jam in Kuala Lumpar, Malaysia – it has seen a 12% increase in road deaths over the past 10 years

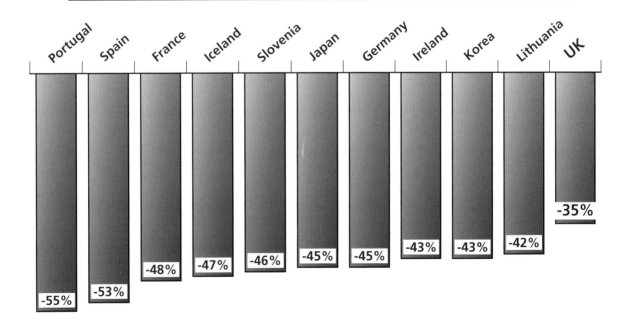

The ten countries with the highest % drop in traffic related deaths, 2000-2009 (UK shown for comparison)

Portugal -55%
Spain -53%
France -48%
Iceland -47%
Slovenia -46%
Japan -45%
Germany -45%
Ireland -43%
Korea -43%
Lithuania -42%
UK -35%

Source: International Transport Forum –
International Road Traffic and Accident Database (IRTAD)
www.internationaltransportforum.org

Cycle of destruction

Despite the reduction in the number of overall road deaths, there was a significant rise in motorcycle deaths in many countries

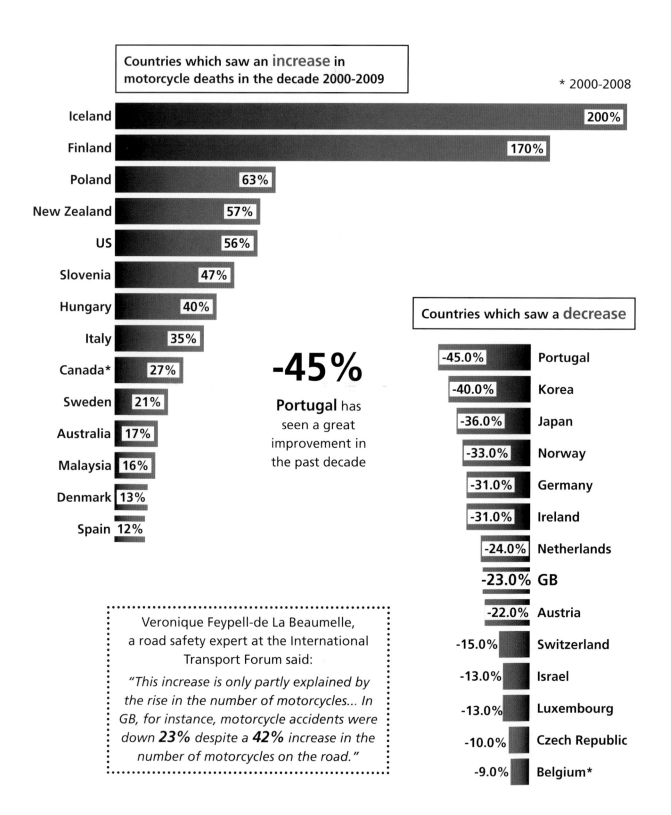

Countries which saw an **increase** in motorcycle deaths in the decade 2000-2009

* 2000-2008

Iceland	200%
Finland	170%
Poland	63%
New Zealand	57%
US	56%
Slovenia	47%
Hungary	40%
Italy	35%
Canada*	27%
Sweden	21%
Australia	17%
Malaysia	16%
Denmark	13%
Spain	12%

-45%

Portugal has seen a great improvement in the past decade

Countries which saw a **decrease**

-45.0%	Portugal
-40.0%	Korea
-36.0%	Japan
-33.0%	Norway
-31.0%	Germany
-31.0%	Ireland
-24.0%	Netherlands
-23.0%	GB
-22.0%	Austria
-15.0%	Switzerland
-13.0%	Israel
-13.0%	Luxembourg
-10.0%	Czech Republic
-9.0%	Belgium*

Veronique Feypell-de La Beaumelle, a road safety expert at the International Transport Forum said:

*"This increase is only partly explained by the rise in the number of motorcycles... In GB, for instance, motorcycle accidents were down **23%** despite a **42%** increase in the number of motorcycles on the road."*

Motorcycle deaths increased in many of the countries covered by the International Traffic Safety Data and Analysis Group (IRTAD)

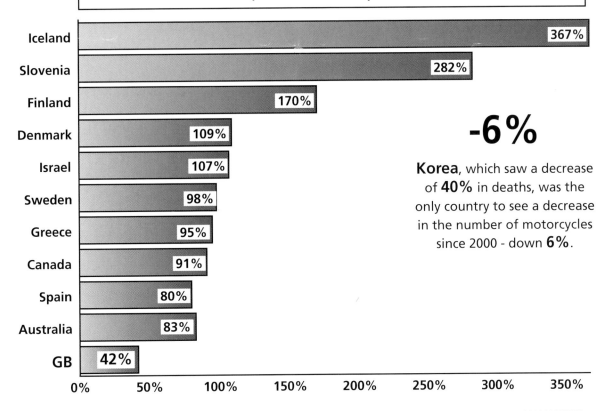

Countries with the highest percentage rise in number of motorcycles, 2000-2009 (GB shown for comparison)

Country	Percentage
Iceland	367%
Slovenia	282%
Finland	170%
Denmark	109%
Israel	107%
Sweden	98%
Greece	95%
Canada	91%
Spain	80%
Australia	83%
GB	42%

-6%

Korea, which saw a decrease of **40%** in deaths, was the only country to see a decrease in the number of motorcycles since 2000 - down **6%**.

The UN has declared 2011 to 2020 the **Decade of Action for Road Safety,** aiming to reduce global road deaths.

www.makeroadssafe.org

Source: International Transport Forum (IRTAD database)
www.internationaltransportforum.org

SEE ALSO:
www.completeissues.co.uk

Travel trends

The recession continued to affect where Brits go for their holidays...

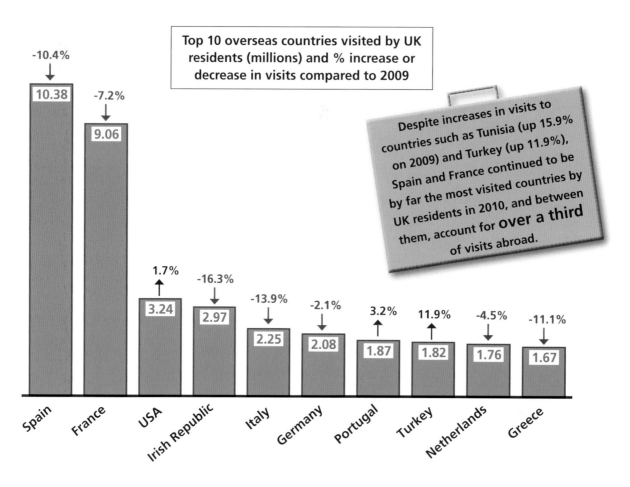

Top 10 overseas countries visited by UK residents (millions) and % increase or decrease in visits compared to 2009

Despite increases in visits to countries such as Tunisia (up 15.9% on 2009) and Turkey (up 11.9%), Spain and France continued to be by far the most visited countries by UK residents in 2010, and between them, account for **over a third** of visits abroad.

Country	Visits (millions)	% change
Spain	10.38	-10.4%
France	9.06	-7.2%
USA	3.24	1.7%
Irish Republic	2.97	-16.3%
Italy	2.25	-13.9%
Germany	2.08	-2.1%
Portugal	1.87	3.2%
Turkey	1.82	11.9%
Netherlands	1.76	-4.5%
Greece	1.67	-11.1%

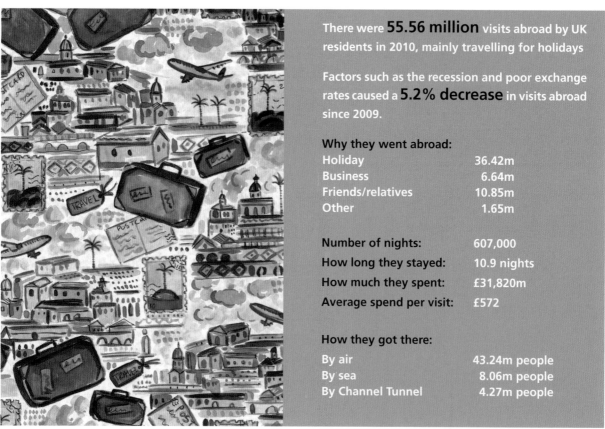

There were **55.56 million** visits abroad by UK residents in 2010, mainly travelling for holidays

Factors such as the recession and poor exchange rates caused a **5.2% decrease** in visits abroad since 2009.

Why they went abroad:

Holiday	36.42m
Business	6.64m
Friends/relatives	10.85m
Other	1.65m

Number of nights:	607,000
How long they stayed:	10.9 nights
How much they spent:	£31,820m
Average spend per visit:	£572

How they got there:

By air	43.24m people
By sea	8.06m people
By Channel Tunnel	4.27m people

...and the numbers coming to Britain

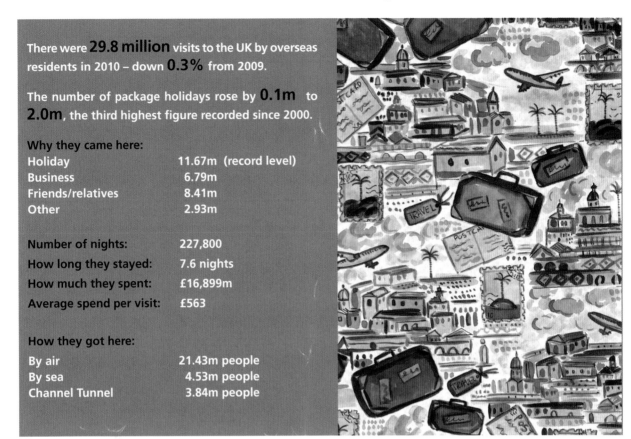

There were **29.8 million** visits to the UK by overseas residents in 2010 – down **0.3%** from 2009.

The number of package holidays rose by **0.1m** to **2.0m**, the third highest figure recorded since 2000.

Why they came here:

Holiday	11.67m (record level)
Business	6.79m
Friends/relatives	8.41m
Other	2.93m

Number of nights:	227,800
How long they stayed:	7.6 nights
How much they spent:	£16,899m
Average spend per visit:	£563

How they got here:

By air	21.43m people
By sea	4.53m people
Channel Tunnel	3.84m people

For many years most visits were made from the USA but in 2010 more were from Europe

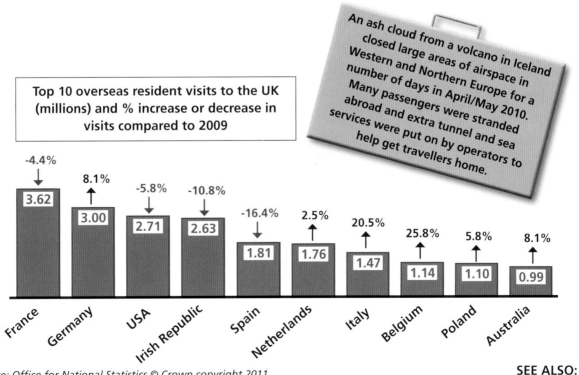

Top 10 overseas resident visits to the UK (millions) and % increase or decrease in visits compared to 2009

An ash cloud from a volcano in Iceland closed large areas of airspace in Western and Northern Europe for a number of days in April/May 2010. Many passengers were stranded abroad and extra tunnel and sea services were put on by operators to help get travellers home.

France	Germany	USA	Irish Republic	Spain	Netherlands	Italy	Belgium	Poland	Australia
-4.4%	8.1%	-5.8%	-10.8%	-16.4%	2.5%	20.5%	25.8%	5.8%	8.1%
3.62	3.00	2.71	2.63	1.81	1.76	1.47	1.14	1.10	0.99

Source: Office for National Statistics © Crown copyright 2011
www.ons.gov.uk

SEE ALSO:
www.completeissues.co.uk

Wish you were here?

Foreign Office staff handled 19,228 serious cases in 2010

If you are a victim of crime of any kind overseas,
the Foreign and Commonwealth Office (FCO)
embassies **may** be able to help you.

What they CAN do:

• issue you with an emergency travel document

• give you a list of local lawyers, interpreters, doctors or funeral directors and help you to contact a local doctor if you need medical treatment

• contact friends and family back home for you

• provide information on how you can safely transfer money from relatives or friends

• visit you in hospital or if you have been arrested

What the FCO CAN'T do:

• help you enter a country if you don't have a valid passport or necessary visas

• give you legal advice

• collect evidence or investigate crimes, or influence the outcome of a trial

• assist with travel costs if you have to attend a trial abroad as a victim or witness

• make travel arrangements for you

• provide general financial help, such as paying any bills or giving you money unless there are very exceptional circumstances

• get you better treatment in hospital or prison than is given to local people

Hospital

Despite fewer people from the UK travelling abroad last year, the number of Brits ending up in hospital abroad has increased to 3,752 with 1,024 of these cases being in Spain.

Proportionally Brits are most likely to be hospitalised in Thailand.

Death

There were 5,972 assistance cases concerning death – 55% of these deaths were from natural causes as opposed to accident, murder or suicide.

Rape

There were 115 rape cases – 19 were in Spain and of the 163 cases of sexual assault 33 were in Spain

Passports

There were 25,969 cases of lost and stolen passports

Top 10 countries where British nationals required assistance 2010/11

Country	Number
Spain	4,971
USA	1,673
France	1,283
Thailand	967
Greece	797
Germany	670
Cyprus	562
Turkey	454
Australia	443
Portugal	418

Although Spain continues to be the country where most Britons require assistance – when you take visitor and resident numbers into account, you are most likely to need consular assistance in the Philippines, Thailand and Pakistan.

Around **66%** of people in Britain don't always find out about the laws of the country they are visiting before they go – putting themselves at risk of breaking the law without realising.

The number of Britons arrested overseas has fallen by over **10%**, but despite this positive trend Foreign Office staff still handled **5,700** arrest cases in 2010/11 – **799** were drug related.

32% of people are not aware that they will always be prosecuted under local law if they break the law abroad

6% of people think they will be prosecuted under UK law and

22% think it depends on the country they are in

4% admit to not knowing at all.

The FCO **Know Before You Go** campaign encourages us to prepare for foreign travel by:

- getting comprehensive travel insurance
- researching local laws and customs
- finding out about health risks
- checking your passport and whether visas are needed
- making copies of important travel documents
- telling someone where you are going and leaving emergency contact details
- taking enough money and having access to emergency funds

Source: British Behaviour Abroad © Crown copyright 2011
www.fco.gov.uk/travel

Fact File 2012 • www.carelpress.com

Travel & transport 155

Give mums a break

Mums end up being just as busy on holiday as they are when they're at home

Nearly 10% say they don't even enjoy their family holiday

TOP TEN CHORES MUMS DO ON HOLIDAY

1. HANG UP CLOTHES TO DRY
2. UNPACK FOR EVERYONE
3. TIDY UP
4. SHOP FOR FOOD
5. PREPARE BREAKFAST
6. VACUUM
7. PREPARE LUNCH
8. CLEAN BATHROOM
9. DO LAUNDRY
10. CHANGE SHEETS

50% get cross about the work they end up doing but say that it's an inevitable part of the family holiday

Nearly **50%** of mums end up preparing meals while they are away.

Instead of relaxing round the pool or on the beach with their family, **33%** of mums often find themselves picking up and cleaning up after their family instead.

Nearly **33%** clean the bathroom everyday despite being on holiday with most saying that no one would do it otherwise.

20% end up ironing which is why **54%** say they try to book all inclusive holidays in the hope that it will give them more of a break.

5% find themselves babysitting the kids while other adults go off and enjoy themselves.

40% found holidays stressful as they still took the responsibility for unpacking, doing washing and preparing meals for their family.

As well as running around after their family **25%** also worry about the jobs they have left behind and end up checking work emails.

40% vacuum and **30%** say they change the bed sheets.

40% feel like their family takes advantage of them when they are on holiday.

Base: Survey of 2,000 mums

Source: Splash About
www.splashabout.net

SEE ALSO:
Who's busiest, p190
www.completeissues.co.uk

War &
conflict

Forced to flee

The number of displaced people is continuing to rise

Internally Displaced Persons (IDPs) are people who have been forced to flee or leave where they usually live because of armed conflict, violence, human rights abuses or natural disasters, but they have remained within their own country

The number of people internally displaced around the world has steadily increased from around

17 million
in 1997 to

27.5 million
by the end of 2010

This is an increase of about

400,000
since the end of 2009.

Over half the world's IDPs were in five countries:
Colombia, Sudan, Iraq, the Democratic Republic of Congo (DRC) and Somalia

All had at least **one million** IDPs.

The **region** with the most IDPs was Africa with **11.1 million** – **40%** of the **world's** IDPs. Over 40% of those in Africa were in **Sudan.**

In **Somalia** and **Sudan**, more than **10%** of the population were internally displaced, and in **Iraq** and **Colombia**, almost **10%**

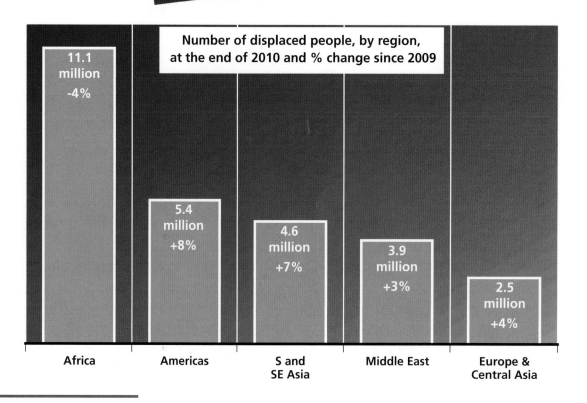

Number of displaced people, by region, at the end of 2010 and % change since 2009

Africa	11.1 million -4%
Americas	5.4 million +8%
S and SE Asia	4.6 million +7%
Middle East	3.9 million +3%
Europe & Central Asia	2.5 million +4%

Largest internally displaced populations

Country	IDPs at end of 2010
Colombia	3.6 million to 5.2 million
Sudan	4.5 million to 5.2 million
Iraq	About 2.8 million
Democratic Republic of the Congo	About 1.7 million
Somalia	About 1.5 million
Pakistan	At least 980,000

The changes in the numbers of IDPs in these six countries over the past 10 years reflect the ongoing conflicts there.

At least **2.9 million** people were **newly displaced** and at least **2.1 million** people **returned** during 2010

Earthquakes and floods were the main natural disasters causing **new displacement** in 2010.

The **Haiti** earthquake in January 2010 displaced **over 1.5 million** people, **over 800,000** of these were **still** in IDP camps at the end of 2010.

In countries such as **Pakistan** and **Colombia**, people already displaced by conflict or violence were among those affected, and often displaced again by floods.

New displacements and numbers returning

Country	New displacements in 2010	Returns in 2010
Africa	1.2 million	At least 959,000
Americas	395,000	No info
S & SE Asia	794,000	At least 660,000
Middle East	177,000	At least 212,000
Europe & Central Asia	300,000	At least 227,000

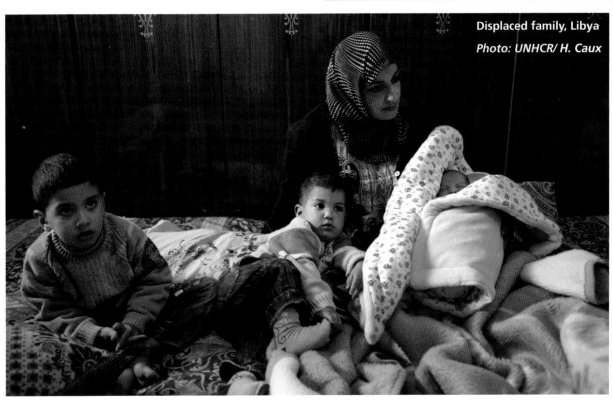

Displaced family, Libya
Photo: UNHCR/ H. Caux

Source: Global developments in 2010, Internal Displacement Monitoring Centre www.internal-displacement.org

SEE ALSO:
Barriers to education, p160
Displaced by disaster p178, Fact File 2011
www.completeissues.co.uk

Barriers to education

Millennium Development Goal 2:
Achieve universal primary education...
...but we are not likely to achieve this – especially in countries affected by conflict

 MDG2 Target: Ensure that by 2015, children everywhere, boys and girls alike, will be able to complete a full course of primary schooling

Countries affected by conflict	Number of primary-aged children out of school 2010
Afghanistan	1,816,000
Angola	824,000
Burundi	244,000
Cambodia	220,000
Central African Republic	310,000
Chad	1,186,000
Colombia	413,000
Côte d'Ivoire	1,164,000
Democratic Republic of Congo	5,203,000
Eritrea	349,000
Ethiopia	3,721,000
Guinea	362,000
Haiti	706,000
Iraq	508,000
Liberia	447,000
Myanmar (Burma)	16,000
Nepal	714,000
Nigeria	8,221,000
Pakistan	6,821,000
Republic of Congo	244,000
Rwanda	88,000
Sierra Leone	285,000
Somalia	1,280,000
Sri Lanka	51,000
Sudan	2,798,000
Timor Leste	71,000
Uganda	341,000
Zimbabwe	281,000
TOTAL	**38,684,000**

More than half of all children who are out of school in the world today live in **conflict-affected fragile states (CAFS)** –

39 million

children out of a total of

72 million

children who are not in school

Children and schools are increasingly the specific targets of violence in CAFS or caught in the crossfire

"The Taliban beat my father and now he cannot work. My brother and I have to work instead of him, and can't go to school. When I see other children go to school I feel happy for them, but I feel very sad for myself."

An out-of-school boy in Afghanistan

This Afghan girl has just started school and is the first in her family to receive an education

Photo: Tracing Tea / Shutterstock.com

Some barriers to education

Poverty:

On average **1 child in 3** in conflict affected countries does not go to school compared with **1 in 11** in other low-income countries. In some countries the figure is even higher – in **Somalia,** and **Afghanistan, more than 80%** of children are out of school.

In almost all CAFS there are fees for primary education. As teachers rely on school fees for their living, they turn children away who can't pay.

Not enough schools:

Many have been destroyed or damaged, or fallen into disrepair because of lack of funds. For children living in rural areas, particularly girls, school is often too far away and too unsafe to reach for fear of landmines, armed attacks, rape and abduction.

In **Afghanistan 50%** of classes are still held in tents or open spaces.

Not enough teachers:

Nearly half of the **37 countries** facing severe primary teacher gaps are CAFS and more than **two-thirds** are in sub-Saharan Africa.

Years of missed schooling:

With conflicts lasting on average ten years, children in CAFS are out of school for all or most of their primary years.

In addition to the **39 million** out of school primary aged children in CAFS, there are millions more older children and young people who have had little or no primary education.

Forced to flee:

Globally there are **18.5 million** children in CAFS who have been forced to leave their homes to escape violence – and are unlikely to return for 17 years.

SEE ALSO:
A war against women, p194, Essential Articles 13
Education inequality, p162, Fact File 2010
www.completeissues.co.uk

Source: The Future Is Now © International Save the Children Alliance 2010
www.savethechildren.net

Fact File 2012 • **www.carelpress.com**

War & conflict **161**

Dangerous waters

On the high seas off the coast of Somalia, heavily armed pirates are overpowering ocean-going fishing or merchant ships to use as a base for further attacks. They capture the crew and force them to sail to within attacking distance of other unsuspecting vessels

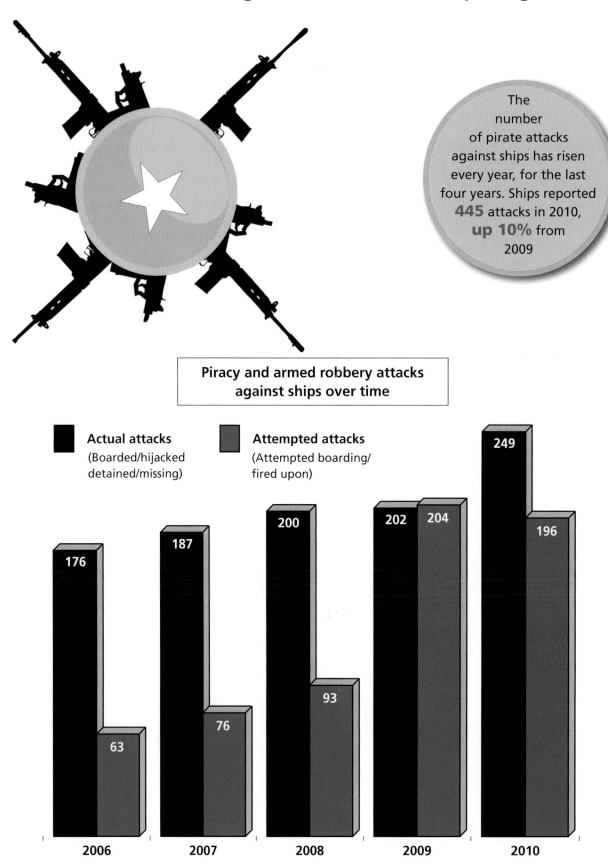

The number of pirate attacks against ships has risen every year, for the last four years. Ships reported **445** attacks in 2010, **up 10%** from 2009

Piracy and armed robbery attacks against ships over time

Actual attacks
(Boarded/hijacked detained/missing)

Attempted attacks
(Attempted boarding/ fired upon)

Year	Actual attacks	Attempted attacks
2006	176	63
2007	187	76
2008	200	93
2009	202	204
2010	249	196

Total incidents per region January to December 2010

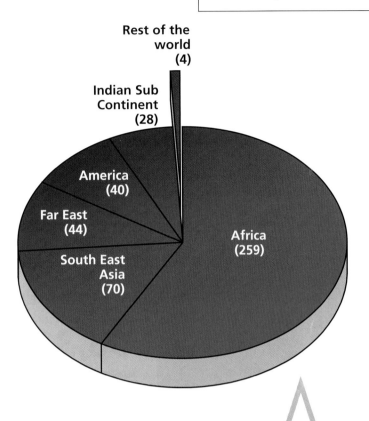

Rest of the world (4)

Indian Sub Continent (28)

America (40)

Far East (44)

South East Asia (70)

Africa (259)

Nearly **75%** of the **445** attacks reported were in just **7** locations in the following regions:

Africa
Somalia **139**
Gulf of Aden **53**
Red Sea... ....**25**
Nigeria.... ....**19**

S E Asia
Indonesia **40**

Far East
South China Sea.... .**31**

Indian Sub Continent
Bangladesh.. ....**23**

The figures for the number of hostages and vessels taken in 2010 were the highest ever seen.

53 ships were hijacked. Pirates captured **1,181** seafarers and killed **8**.

Attacks in the Gulf of Aden region more than halved in 2010 because of naval presence protecting ships.

Worldwide incidents as at 21/10/11

Total attacks **369**
Total hijackings **36**

Vessels held by Somali pirates
Vessels **13**
Hostages **249**

During 2011, in a new cross-border strategy, Somali pirates kidnapped people from luxury beach resorts in Kenya.

October 2011:

The Prime Minister announced that ships sailing under a British flag would be able to carry armed guards to protect them from pirates.

The International Chamber of Shipping (ICS), which represents over 80% of the world's merchant fleet, welcomed the move as a deterrent – but said it was only a 'short-term measure'.

The ICS was concerned for the impact on crews if the pirates responded with increased firepower.

Source: Piracy and armed robbery against ships 2010 report, © International Chamber Of Commerce, International Maritime Bureau Piracy Reporting Centre, 2011

www.icc-ccs.org

War & peace

For the third year running the world is less peaceful

How do we measure peace?

The *Global Peace Index (GPI)* measures ongoing conflict inside countries and between countries, safety and security in society and military build-up in the country.

It ranks 153 nations according to their 'absence of violence'.

It recorded increases in a number of areas eg the threat of terrorist attacks in 29 nations and greater likelihood of violent demonstrations in 33 countries.

Western Europe remains the most peaceful region, with most of the countries ranking in the top 20 overall.

Most peaceful

1	Iceland
2	New Zealand
3	Japan
4	Denmark
5	Czech Republic
6	Austria
7	Finland
8	Canada
9	Norway
10	Slovenia
26	UK

Least peaceful

144	Central African Republic
145	Israel
146	Pakistan
147	Russia
148	Democratic Republic of Congo
149	North Korea
150	Afghanistan
151	Sudan
152	Iraq
153	Somalia

The series of protests and demonstrations across the Middle East and North Africa known as the 'Arab Spring' had a dramatic effect on rankings, causing **Libya** to drop **83 places** to **143rd,** **Bahrain** to drop **51 places** to **123rd** and Egypt to drop **24 places** to **73rd.**

Sub-Saharan Africa remains the region least at peace, containing **40%** of the world's least peaceful countries.

Source: Global Peace Index Rankings 2011
www.visionofhumanity.org

SEE ALSO:
Conflicting countries, p154, Fact File 2010

www.completeissues.co.uk

Wider world

Promises, promises

In 2010, development aid to sub-Saharan Africa was the highest on record but still fell short of the commitments made in 2005

The 'Make Poverty History' summit held at Gleneagles in 2005, placed a special emphasis on sub-Saharan Africa, the region furthest from achieving the eight *Millennium Development Goals* – these range from halving extreme poverty to halting the spread of HIV/AIDS and providing universal primary education, all by the target date of 2015.

The G7 countries* increased their annual development aid to sub-Saharan Africa by **$11.197 billion** between 2004 and 2010 but this represented only **61%** of the **$18.227** billion increases they promised in 2005. This was because of a shortfall from Italy, Germany and France.

The UK's progress

Between 2004 and 2010, the UK increased its development assistance to sub-Saharan Africa by **$2.55 billion** (£1.65bn) more than doubling the assistance to the region from the 2004 levels.

It delivered a total of **$5.06 billion** (£3.28bn) in 2010 meeting **85%** of its target increases.

The UK's 2015 target for development assistance to sub-Saharan Africa is **$9.05 billion** (£5.86bn).

*Seven of the world's leading industrialised nations – Canada, France, Germany, Italy, Japan, UK and the US.

The G7's promises compared to actual increases

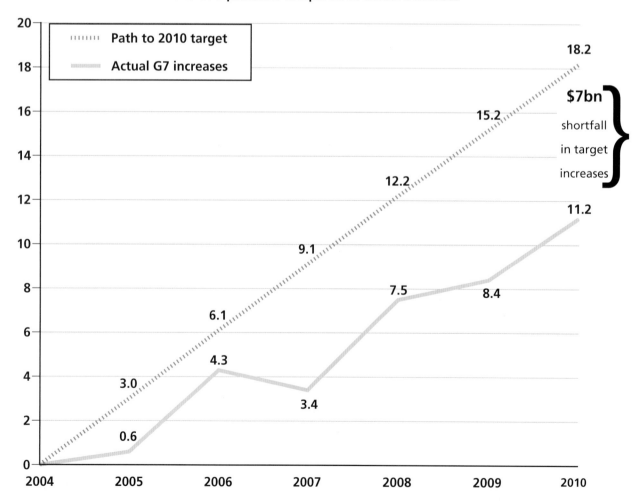

Legend:
- Path to 2010 target
- Actual G7 increases

Path to 2010 target values: 3.0, 6.1, 9.1, 12.2, 15.2, 18.2

Actual G7 increases values: 0.6, 4.3, 3.4, 7.5, 8.4, 11.2

$7bn shortfall in target increases

Years: 2004, 2005, 2006, 2007, 2008, 2009, 2010

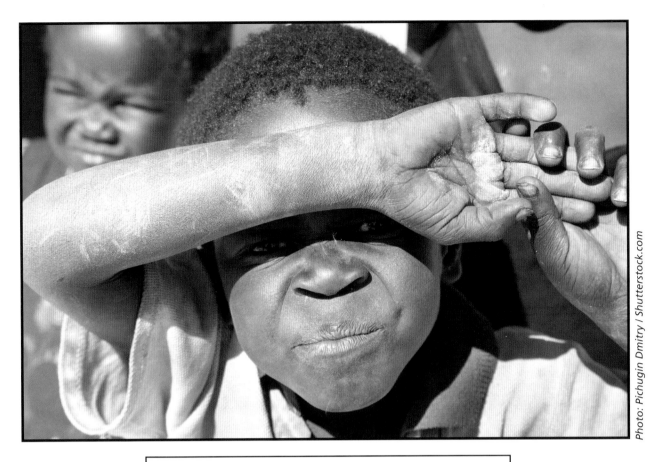

Photo: Pichugin Dmitry / Shutterstock.com

What each person gave to sub-Saharan Africa in 2010, (US dollars)

G7 countries

UK
$222.74

France
$176.89

Germany
$154.62

Canada
$148.77

United States
$97.48

Japan
$86.59

Italy
$47.55

Other selected countries for comparison

Norway
$927.55

Sweden
$480.53

Australia
$171.95

New Zealand
$80.37

South Korea
$23.89

SEE ALSO:
Commitment to development, p172, Fact File 2011
Where your money goes, p174, Fact File 2011

Source: DATA Report 2011, One International
www.one.org/data

www.completeissues.co.uk

Making progress?
Safe drinking water

The world is on track to meet the Millennium Development Goal's drinking water target

In September 2000, 189 countries endorsed the Millennium Declaration, setting out goals to be reached by 2015.

Millennium Development Goal 7 contains the target:
Halve, by 2015, the proportion of people without sustainable access to safe drinking water and basic sanitation

Trends in the use of drinking water sources, by region, 2008

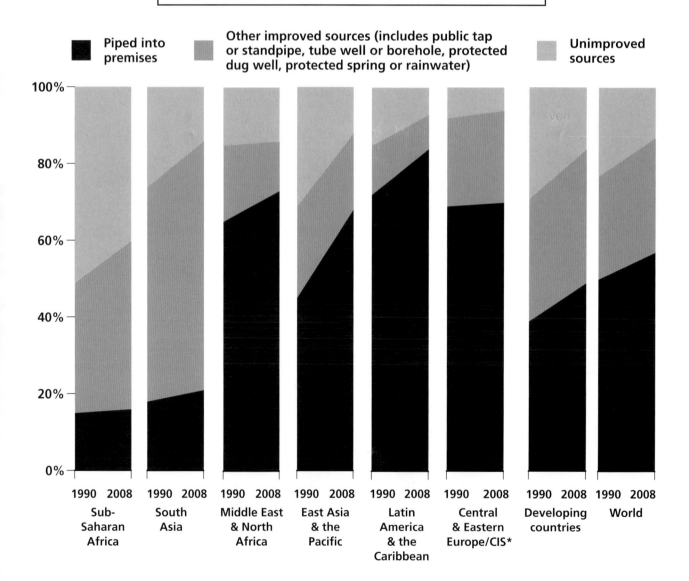

■ Piped into premises

Other improved sources (includes public tap or standpipe, tube well or borehole, protected dug well, protected spring or rainwater)

Unimproved sources

1990 2008 — Sub-Saharan Africa
1990 2008 — South Asia
1990 2008 — Middle East & North Africa
1990 2008 — East Asia & the Pacific
1990 2008 — Latin America & the Caribbean
1990 2008 — Central & Eastern Europe/CIS*
1990 2008 — Developing countries
1990 2008 — World

*Commonwealth of Independent States (former Soviet Union)

Global coverage of safe drinking water increased from **77%** in 1990 to **87%** in 2008, with the East Asia and Pacific region showing the biggest improvement.

Within the **developing world**, access to safe water is not equal between town and country areas.

There are still
884 million
people who lack access to improved drinking water sources, and
84%
of them live in **rural areas**

Of the
1.8 billion
people who have gained access to improved drinking water sources since 1990,
60%
live in urban areas

The largest inequalities are found in Sub-Saharan Africa. In 17 countries, less than half the rural population uses improved drinking water sources.

Even within towns, water is not available equally. In many countries, the poorest **20%** of people living in **urban areas** have significantly lower access to improved drinking water sources than the richest **20%**.

Source: © UNICEF – Progress for Children, September 2010; WHO / UNICEF Joint Monitoring Programme (JMP) for Water Supply and Sanitation
www.unicef.org.uk
www.wssinfo.org

In households that do not have a drinking water source on the premises, who collects the water?

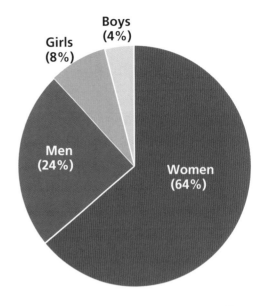

Boys (4%)
Girls (8%)
Men (24%)
Women (64%)

Many trips may be required just to collect enough drinking water for the home each day

SEE ALSO:
www.completeissues.co.uk

Child brides

"Child marriage denies girls their childhood, deprives them of an education and robs them of their innocence"

Ann M. Veneman, UNICEF Executive Director

Photo: © UNICEF/NYHQ2009-2036/Sweeting

Adolescent girls in Cameroon

- The term 'child marriage' is used to refer to both formal marriages and informal unions in which a girl lives with a partner as if married before the age of 18.

- Child marriage is most common in South Asia and sub-Saharan Africa.

- Around **one third** of girls in the developing world, excluding China, are married before the age of 18.

- Most child marriages take place between the ages of 15 and 18, but in Niger, Chad and Bangladesh, more than **one third** of women aged 20-24 were already married by the age of 15.

While child marriage has decreased globally over the last 30 years, it is still common in rural areas and among the poorest of the poor.

Rates of child marriage are about **three times** higher in poorer households than those from the richest.

Parents will often give up their daughters for economic reasons, or believe child marriage will protect their daughters and family status.

Most married adolescent girls will not complete secondary education and many will become pregnant before their bodies are mature enough to safely deliver a child. The more education a girl receives, the more likely she is to postpone marriage and motherhood.

> *"Child marriages are often a result of poverty and ignorance"*
> *Ann M. Veneman, UNICEF Executive Director*

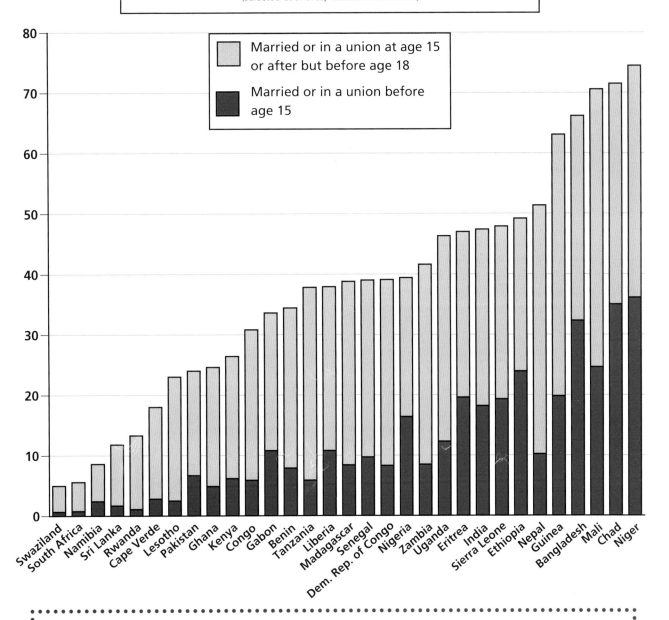

Percentage of women aged 20-24 who were first married or in a union by age 15 and 18, South Asia and sub-Saharan Africa

(selected countries, latest available data)

Legend:
- Married or in a union at age 15 or after but before age 18
- Married or in a union before age 15

Countries (left to right): Swaziland, South Africa, Namibia, Sri Lanka, Rwanda, Cape Verde, Lesotho, Pakistan, Ghana, Kenya, Congo, Gabon, Benin, Tanzania, Liberia, Madagascar, Senegal, Dem. Rep. of Congo, Nigeria, Zambia, Uganda, Eritrea, India, Sierra Leone, Ethiopia, Nepal, Guinea, Bangladesh, Mali, Chad, Niger

In places where child marriage is practised, girls rarely have any say in when and whom they marry

In Yemen on 24th July 2009, Nojoud Ali succeeded in divorcing her 30-year-old husband... she was just 10-years-old.

Fawziya Youssef from Yemen died in childbirth in September 2009. She was forced into a marriage with a man at least twice her age and became pregnant.

Both she and her baby died after she was in labour for three days... she was 12-years-old.

In Yemen the legal age for marriage is currently 15, but in reality, parents can decide that their daughter should marry when she is much younger.

The average age for marriage in rural Yemen is around 12 or 13.

Sources: State of the World's Children 2011
Childmatters, Spring 2011, Childinfo, February 2011 © UNICEF
www.unicef.org/sowc
www.childinfo.org

SEE ALSO:
Child birth, p178
www.completeissues.co.uk

Child birth

About 16 million adolescent girls aged 15-19 give birth each year. This is more than 10% of all births worldwide

The younger a girl is when she becomes pregnant, the greater the risks to her health. Girls under 15 are **5 times** more likely to die in childbirth and pregnancy than those aged 20-24.

Girls aged 15 to 19 are **twice** as likely to die. Most of these deaths are girls who are married.

At least **2.5 million** adolescent pregnancies each year lead to unsafe abortions

Complications from unsafe abortions are the leading cause of death among teenagers in many countries in southern and eastern Africa and Latin America

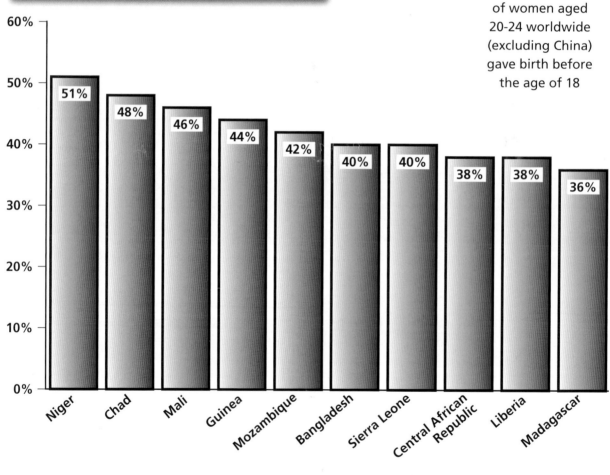

Countries with the highest percentage of women aged 20-24 who gave birth before age 18
2009 or latest available date

20% of women aged 20-24 worldwide (excluding China) gave birth before the age of 18

Adolescent pregnancy is dangerous:

Mothers aged 10 to 19 account for **11%** of all births worldwide but **23%** of the overall burden of disease due to pregnancy and childbirth.

It is also dangerous for the child:

Stillbirths and death in the first week of life are **50%** higher among babies born to mothers younger than 20 than among mothers aged 20 to 29. Rates of premature birth, low birth weight and asphyxia (lack of oxygen) are higher among children born to mothers under 18.

In 2008
the **worldwide**
birth rate for girls
aged 15-19 was

51

per 1,000 girls

In the **UK**
the rate was

26

births per 1,000 girls
aged 15-19

In low and middle
income countries,
almost **10%** of
girls become mothers
by age 16

**Countries with the highest number of births
per 1,000 girls aged 15-19**

2008 or latest available date

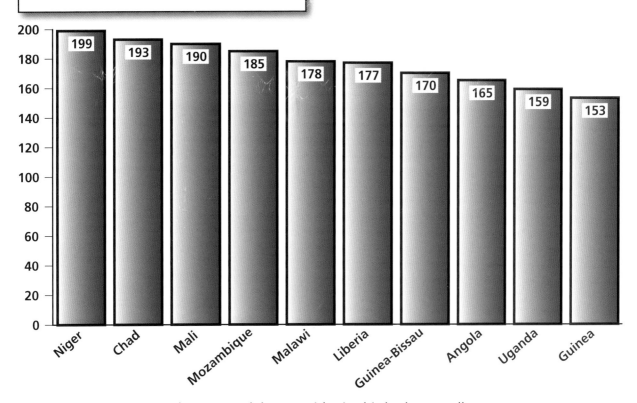

When poor adolescent girls give birth, they usually
pass on their situation of poverty and inequality
to their children. For those with low levels of
education, this cycle is even more difficult to escape.

*Source: State of the World's Children 2011; UNFPA
Fact Sheet: Young People and Times of Change;
World Health Organization*
www.unicef.org/sowc
www.unfpa.org/public/home/factsheets/pid/3851
www.who.int

SEE ALSO:
Full stop, p134
Child brides, p176
Baby mothers, p62, Fact File 2010
www.completeissues.co.uk

Missing midwives

Every year, 48 million women give birth without someone with the right skills. More than 2 million women give birth completely alone

1,000 women and **2,000 babies** die every day from birth complications which could be easily prevented.

There is a global shortage of midwives. If there were **350,000** more midwives many mothers would be saved and **1.3 million** newborn babies would survive every year.

Women in the poorest countries are:

- least likely to have a skilled person with them during birth
- more likely to lose their newborn
- most likely to die themselves during childbirth.

The World Health Organization recommends one midwife or skilled birth attendant for every **175** pregnant women but this standard is far from being achieved. In Rwanda for example, where **400,000** babies are born in a year, there are 46 midwives – one for every **8,600** births.

Worldwide,

35%

of pregnant women give birth without a midwife or a skilled birth attendant. In some countries rates of unattended births are much higher.

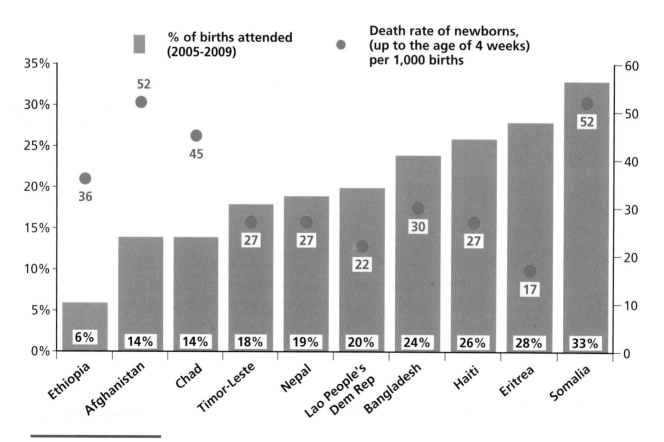

Ten countries with the lowest rates of skilled birth attendance

- % of births attended (2005-2009)
- Death rate of newborns, (up to the age of 4 weeks) per 1,000 births

Country	% of births attended	Death rate
Ethiopia	6%	36
Afghanistan	14%	52
Chad	14%	45
Timor-Leste	18%	27
Nepal	19%	27
Lao People's Dem Rep	20%	22
Bangladesh	24%	30
Haiti	26%	27
Eritrea	28%	17
Somalia	33%	52

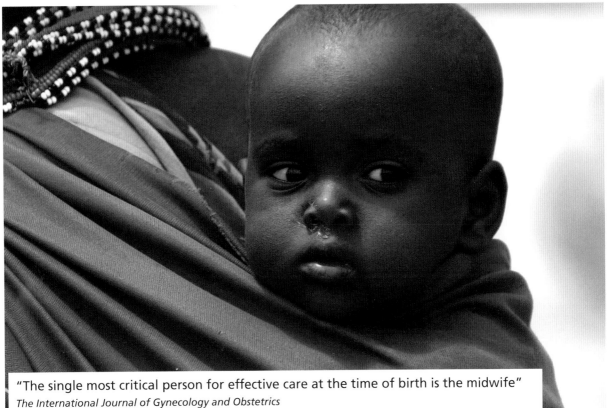

"The single most critical person for effective care at the time of birth is the midwife"
The International Journal of Gynecology and Obstetrics

The ten loneliest places to give birth

latest available figures

Country	% of women giving birth alone
Nigeria	18.6%
Niger	16.9%
Mali	13.1%
Rwanda	11.1%
Guinea	9.0%
Uganda	8.9%
Angola	8.4%
Kenya	6.5%
Nepal	6.3%
Ethiopia	5.4%

On average, in the
least developed countries

59%

of births have no midwife or skilled health worker present: in **Ethiopia** the figure is **94%** of births and in **Bangladesh 76%**.

By comparison, only **1%** of women in the **UK** give birth without a midwife or skilled birth attendant, usually because the birth is so fast the woman can't get to hospital.

There is some progress even in poor and war-torn countries. Afghanistan is one of the most dangerous places in the world to be born, but the number of midwives, although very low, has tripled within the past 3 years, thanks, in part, to aid agencies such as Save the Children

Recruiting, training and supporting midwives is critical to the achievement of the
Millennium Development Goals 4 and 5 to reduce child deaths by two-thirds
and maternal mortality by three-quarters.

SEE ALSO:
Women & children first, p160, Fact File 2010

Source: Save the Children Missing Midwives Report 2011
www.savethechildren.org.uk

www.completeissues.co.uk

AIDS orphans

Even though HIV worldwide has declined and more people have access to treatment, the total number of children who have lost their parents due to HIV has not gone down

By the end of 2009,
the AIDS epidemic had left behind

16.6 million

AIDS orphans.

Almost **90%** live in Sub-Saharan Africa.

9 million

AIDS orphans live in just six countries – Kenya, Nigeria, South Africa, Uganda, United Republic of Tanzania and Zimbabwe.

Nigeria alone has **2.5 million** orphans.

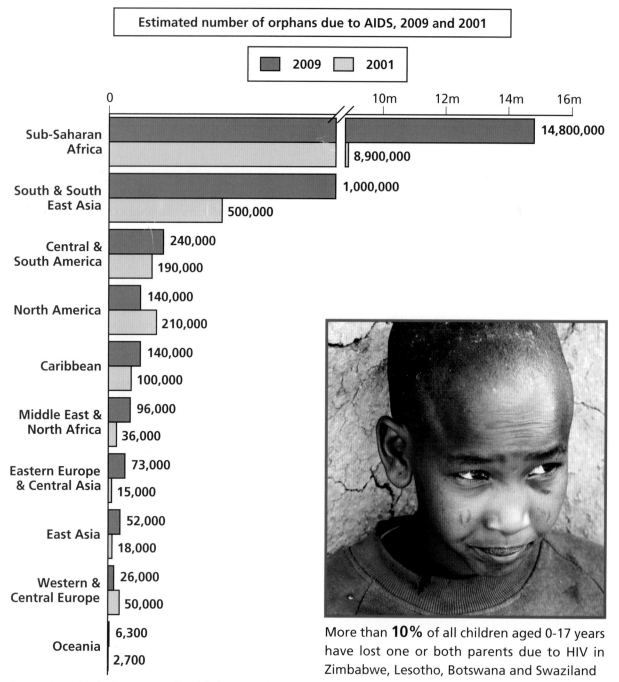

| Estimated number of orphans due to AIDS, 2009 and 2001 |

■ 2009   □ 2001

	2009	2001
Sub-Saharan Africa	14,800,000	8,900,000
South & South East Asia	1,000,000	500,000
Central & South America	240,000	190,000
North America	140,000	210,000
Caribbean	140,000	100,000
Middle East & North Africa	96,000	36,000
Eastern Europe & Central Asia	73,000	15,000
East Asia	52,000	18,000
Western & Central Europe	26,000	50,000
Oceania	6,300	2,700

More than **10%** of all children aged 0-17 years have lost one or both parents due to HIV in Zimbabwe, Lesotho, Botswana and Swaziland

Source: Avert; UNAIDS Report on the Global AIDS epidemic © 2010
www.avert.org/worldstatinfo.htm
www.unaids.org

SEE ALSO:
www.completeissues.co.uk

Work

Workless

The number of households with no-one in work has declined, but there are more people who have NEVER worked

Percentage of UK households working, mixed and workless

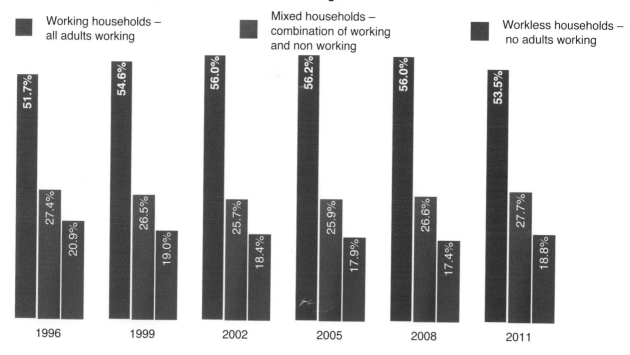

- Working households – all adults working
- Mixed households – combination of working and non working
- Workless households – no adults working

1996: 51.7% | 27.4% | 20.9%
1999: 54.6% | 26.5% | 19.0%
2002: 56.0% | 25.7% | 18.4%
2005: 56.2% | 25.9% | 17.9%
2008: 56.0% | 26.6% | 17.4%
2011: 53.5% | 27.7% | 18.8%

Percentage of workless households by region

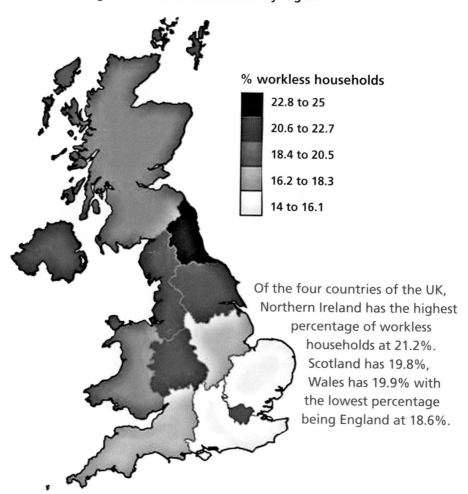

% workless households
- 22.8 to 25
- 20.6 to 22.7
- 18.4 to 20.5
- 16.2 to 18.3
- 14 to 16.1

Of the four countries of the UK, Northern Ireland has the highest percentage of workless households at 21.2%. Scotland has 19.8%, Wales has 19.9% with the lowest percentage being England at 18.6%.

There were falls in the percentage of workless households. The largest fall was in single person households with no children. In 2011 around **34.7%** of one-person households were not in work, down **2.1%** on a year earlier. Households without dependent children are more likely to be workless, **21.8%**, compared to **13.7%** of households with dependent children.

Number of households where all those of working age have NEVER worked (thousands)

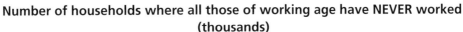
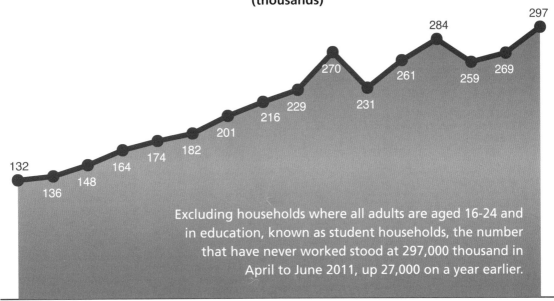

132 · 136 · 148 · 164 · 174 · 182 · 201 · 216 · 229 · 270 · 231 · 261 · 284 · 259 · 269 · 297

Excluding households where all adults are aged 16-24 and in education, known as student households, the number that have never worked stood at 297,000 thousand in April to June 2011, up 27,000 on a year earlier.

1996 1997 1998 1999 2000 2001 2002 2003 2004 2005 2006 2007 2008 2009 2010 2011

Source: Working and workless households 2011 - Summary of key findings © Crown copyright 2011
www.ons.gov.uk

SEE ALSO:
Rush-hour silence in a welfare ghetto, p199, Essential Articles 14
A poor start, p100, Essential Articles 12
www.completeissues.co.uk

Class of 2011

Graduates are scrambling for jobs

> Graduates leaving Britain's top universities in 2011 made around **343,000** job applications, **33%** more than in 2010.

> On average each student made **6.8** applications – a rise from **5.7** the previous year.

> **37%** applied in September or October 2010 – a record number of early applications.

After graduation, students expected to...

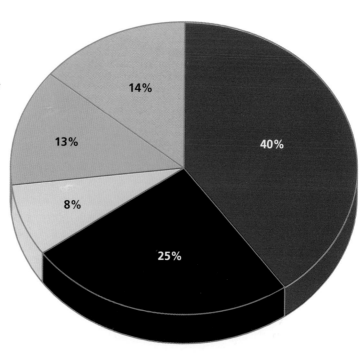

- ■ ...start a graduate job or be looking for a graduate job after leaving university

- ■ ...remain at university to study for a postgraduate course

- ▢ ...take temporary or voluntary work

- ▢ ...take time off or go travelling

- ▢ Yet to decide what to do next

Pie chart values: 40%, 25%, 8%, 13%, 14%

In previous years the average starting salary had increased. For example 2010 salaries were **7.4%** higher than 2009. In 2011, salaries are likely to remain unchanged from the level in 2010 – an average (median) of **£29,000.**

But research showed that the salaries on offer varied considerably from organisation to organisation – for example, outside the City of London, the highest salary was at *Aldi*, which paid graduates training to become area managers a first-year salary of **£40,000**.

Graduate salaries at UK employers in 2011, by sector

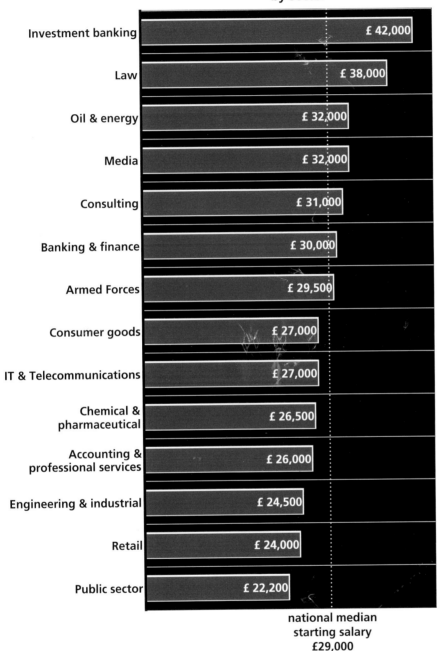

Investment banking	£ 42,000
Law	£ 38,000
Oil & energy	£ 32,000
Media	£ 32,000
Consulting	£ 31,000
Banking & finance	£ 30,000
Armed Forces	£ 29,500
Consumer goods	£ 27,000
IT & Telecommunications	£ 27,000
Chemical & pharmaceutical	£ 26,500
Accounting & professional services	£ 26,000
Engineering & industrial	£ 24,500
Retail	£ 24,000
Public sector	£ 22,200

national median starting salary £29,000

For the first time since 2008, investment banking was attracting more applications from final year students than any other career area.

***

Overall, the most popular career areas were expected to be in the media, teaching and marketing.

Although the total number of graduate vacancies was set to increase in 2011, **a third** of these positions were expected to be filled by graduates who had already worked for the organisations in industrial placements and internships, vacation work or sponsorships. Therefore they would not be open to other students from the *Class of 2011*.

The UK Graduate Careers Survey 2011 was based on interviews with 17,851 final year students from thirty leading universities

Source: UK Graduate Careers Survey 2011, The Graduate Market in 2011, High Fliers Research Ltd www.highfliers.co.uk

SEE ALSO:
Poor prospects... p194,
Essential Articles 14
www.completeissues.co.uk

Missing women

More women than ever are working, but they are not making it to the top

Women make up **51%** of the British population. Young, well-educated women are entering the labour market and reaching the ranks of middle management. Over **45%** of solicitors are now women and it is predicted there will be more female than male doctors by **2017**.

However, these changes are not yet reflected in the senior ranks, even in occupations where women have a long history of representation. For example, women account for the majority of full-time teachers but just over a third of secondary school head teachers.

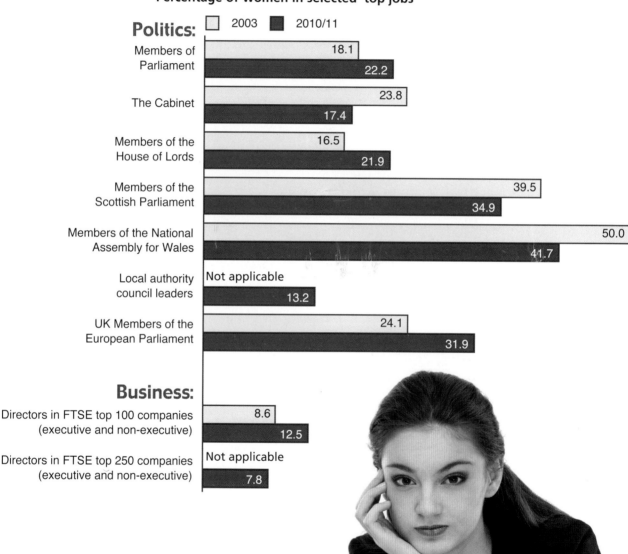

Percentage of women in selected 'top jobs'

2003 | 2010/11

Politics:

Members of Parliament
- 2003: 18.1
- 2010/11: 22.2

The Cabinet
- 2003: 23.8
- 2010/11: 17.4

Members of the House of Lords
- 2003: 16.5
- 2010/11: 21.9

Members of the Scottish Parliament
- 2003: 39.5
- 2010/11: 34.9

Members of the National Assembly for Wales
- 2003: 50.0
- 2010/11: 41.7

Local authority council leaders
- 2003: Not applicable
- 2010/11: 13.2

UK Members of the European Parliament
- 2003: 24.1
- 2010/11: 31.9

Business:

Directors in FTSE top 100 companies (executive and non-executive)
- 2003: 8.6
- 2010/11: 12.5

Directors in FTSE top 250 companies (executive and non-executive)
- 2003: Not applicable
- 2010/11: 7.8

Why:

In large companies, where long working hours are the norm, women struggle more than men to get ahead. Currently women are still responsible for the majority of domestic chores and childcare duties. The mixture of inflexible working hours at big organisations and bearing the bulk of domestic responsibility limits women's route to the top.

Public & voluntary sectors:

Percentage of women in selected 'top jobs'

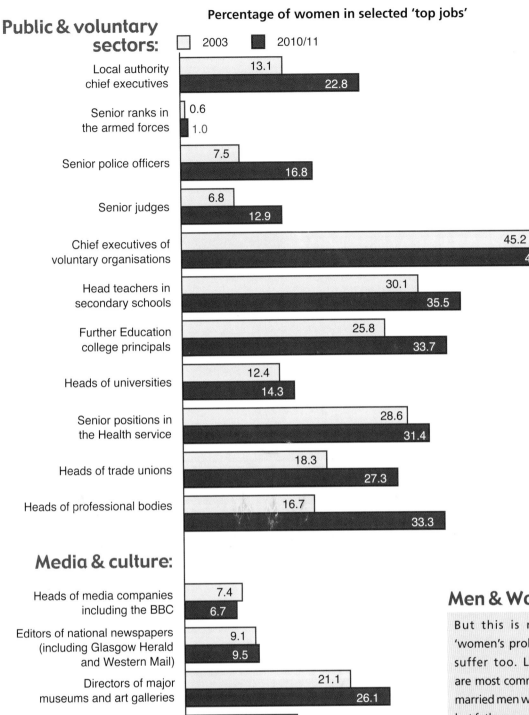

☐ 2003   ■ 2010/11

Job	2003	2010/11
Local authority chief executives	13.1	22.8
Senior ranks in the armed forces	0.6	1.0
Senior police officers	7.5	16.8
Senior judges	6.8	12.9
Chief executives of voluntary organisations	45.2	48.0
Head teachers in secondary schools	30.1	35.5
Further Education college principals	25.8	33.7
Heads of universities	12.4	14.3
Senior positions in the Health service	28.6	31.4
Heads of trade unions	18.3	27.3
Heads of professional bodies	16.7	33.3

Media & culture:

Job	2003	2010/11
Heads of media companies including the BBC	7.4	6.7
Editors of national newspapers (including Glasgow Herald and Western Mail)	9.1	9.5
Directors of major museums and art galleries	21.1	26.1
Chief executives of national sports bodies	14.3	25.0

Men & Women:

But this is not just a 'women's problem'. Men suffer too. Long hours are most common among married men with children, but fathers are increasingly saying that they want to spend more time with their families and less time at work, and they want to play a more equal part in childcare.

Equality:

To achieve equal numbers of women as men, at the current rate of progress it will take:

Senior Police Officers: **30 years**

Directors in the FTSE **100: 70 years**

Senior Judges: **45 years**

MPs: **14 elections or up to 70 years**

SEE ALSO:
Worlds apart, p174
Is the new woman's place in the home?
p196, Essential Articles 14
A woman's place... is in the home?
p182, Fact File 2011
www.completeissues.co.uk

Source: Sex and power 2011, Equality and Human Rights Commission
www.equalityhumanrights.com

Who's busiest?

People spend about a third of their time in paid or unpaid work

The amount of time spent every day on **paid** work or study and **unpaid** work is much higher in Mexico than in some other countries. **Mexicans** spend a total of **10 hours** on work, study or chores.

Belgians spend least time – **7 hours**. The **OECD average** is **8 hours** a day.

Total time spent in paid and unpaid work or study per day, in OECD countries, in hrs:mins

(Averages are based on total population aged 15-64 (working age) – whether they are in paid work or not)

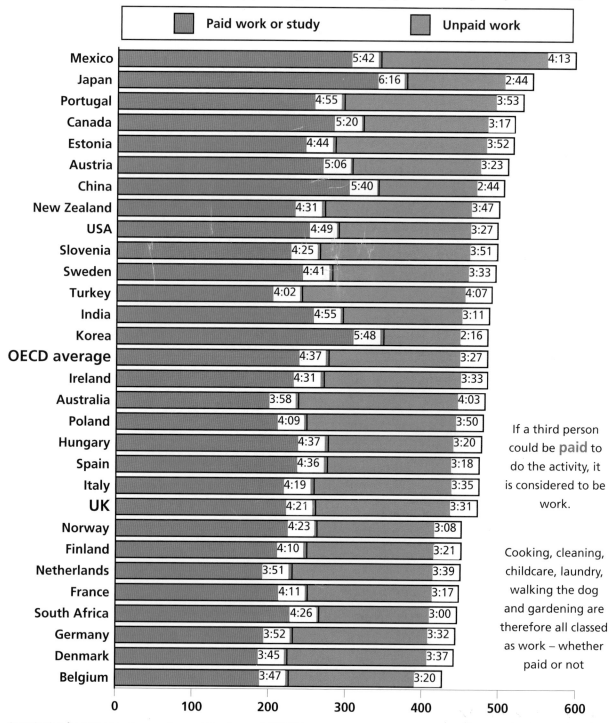

	Paid work or study	Unpaid work
Mexico	5:42	4:13
Japan	6:16	2:44
Portugal	4:55	3:53
Canada	5:20	3:17
Estonia	4:44	3:52
Austria	5:06	3:23
China	5:40	2:44
New Zealand	4:31	3:47
USA	4:49	3:27
Slovenia	4:25	3:51
Sweden	4:41	3:33
Turkey	4:02	4:07
India	4:55	3:11
Korea	5:48	2:16
OECD average	4:37	3:27
Ireland	4:31	3:33
Australia	3:58	4:03
Poland	4:09	3:50
Hungary	4:37	3:20
Spain	4:36	3:18
Italy	4:19	3:35
UK	4:21	3:31
Norway	4:23	3:08
Finland	4:10	3:21
Netherlands	3:51	3:39
France	4:11	3:17
South Africa	4:26	3:00
Germany	3:52	3:32
Denmark	3:45	3:37
Belgium	3:47	3:20

If a third person could be **paid** to do the activity, it is considered to be work.

Cooking, cleaning, childcare, laundry, walking the dog and gardening are therefore all classed as work – whether paid or not

Organisation for Economic Co-operation and Development (OECD) is an international organisation of 34, mainly high income, developed countries

Gender gap

Whether a country is near the top or the bottom of the rankings for unpaid work, women are doing more

In all countries, **women do more unpaid work than men** – on average **2.5 hours per day**.

There is a significant difference between countries. **Turkish, Mexican and Indian women** spend, per day, **4.3 to 5 hours more**, while the difference is only a little over **one hour** in countries like **Norway, Sweden and Denmark**.

Indian and Mexican gender differences are due to the long hours women spend in the kitchen and caring for children.

In Southern Europe, Korea and Japan, women also do considerably more unpaid work than men.

Women in the **UK** spend **two hours more** per day doing unpaid work than men.

Part of the reason for women's higher share of unpaid work is their shorter time in paid work.

When you add paid and unpaid work there's almost no difference between the genders. Women do less paid work than men but more unpaid work such as housework and caring.

The countries where men do the least unpaid work are **Korea, India and Japan** – where they do less than **one hour**.

It is not always the case that when men do a low amount of unpaid work, women do a high amount. In **China**, for instance, men spend **1 hour 31 minutes** and women spend **3 hours 54 minutes**.

In **Australia** both sexes spend a considerable amount of time on unpaid work: men **2 hours 52 minutes** and women **5 hours 11 minutes**.

Source: Society at a Glance, 2011:
OECD Social Indicators © OECD 2011
www.oecd.org

SEE ALSO:
Work and play, p190, Fact File 2011
www.completeissues.co.uk

Index

Entries in **colour** refer to main sections. Where there are double page spreads the page number refers to the first page.

A

Abuse 56, 58, 176
Adoption 63
Age 138
Aid 168
AIDS see HIV/AIDS
ALCOHOL, DRUGS & SMOKING 7-14
Animals 52, 78, 92

B

Beaches 46
Birth 128, 134, 178, 180
Body image 90
BRITAIN & ITS CITIZENS 15-24 & 54, 120, 124, 138, 140, 142, 146, 152, 184
Bullying 32

C

Cancer 94, 104
Care & carers 63
Charity 70, 168
Child abuse 56, 58, 176
Child care 66
Children 54, 56, 58, 63, 68, 176
Cities 137
Consumers & shopping 42, 44, 78, 80, 84
Cosmetic surgery 90
Crime see **LAW & ORDER 119-126**

D

Death 110, 128, 134, 148, 150
Debt 38, 40, 72, 74, 75
Divorce see Marriage & divorce
Domestic violence 56
Drugs 10, 14

E

Eating disorders 88
EDUCATION 25-40 & 54, 60, 82, 160
Energy 50
ENVIRONMENTAL ISSUES 41-52 & 78
Equality 20, 26, 174, 188

F

Facebook 112, 116
FAMILY & RELATIONSHIPS 53-66 & 8, 12, 38, 68, 112, 116, 156
FINANCIAL ISSUES 67-76 & 22, 38, 40, 42, 54, 66, 80
Fitness 144
FOOD & DRINK 77-86 & 48

G

Gambling 72
Gender 20, 66, 144, 174, 188, 190

H

HEALTH UK 87-100 & 14, 78, 80
HEALTH WORLDWIDE 101-110 & 134, 170, 172, 178, 180, 182
HIV/AIDS 96, 108, 110, 182
Housing 22, 54

I

Immigration 18, 140
INTERNET & MEDIA 111-118

J

Japan 50

L

LAW & ORDER 119-126 & 54, 154, 162
Litter 44, 46

M

Malaria 100, 102
Marriage & divorce 64, 138, 176
Media 36
Mental health, 60, 88
Midwives 180
Mobile phones 114
Motorcycle deaths 150

N

Nationality 16, 140
Nuclear power 50

O

Obesity 84
Olympics 146
Organic food 78, 80

P

Parents 8, 12, 24, 28, 30, 34, 38, 62, 68, 82 see also **FAMILY & RELATIONSHIPS 53-66**
Peace 164, 166
Pirates 162
Pocket money 68
POPULATION 127-140 & 18
Poverty 168
Pregnancy see Birth
Prison 122, 124, 126

R

Race 17
Reading 36
Refugees 158
Religion 17, 34
Riots 120, 126
Road deaths 148, 150

S

Safety & risk 14, 148, 150, 154
Sanitation 172
School meals 82
Sexual abuse 56, 58
Sexual issues 96
Smoking 12, 14
Social networks 112, 116
SPORT & LEISURE 141-146

T

TB 98, 106
Tourism 142, 152, 154, 156
TRAVEL & TRANSPORT 147-156

U

Unemployment 184
United Nations 164
University 38, 40, 186

W

WAR & CONFLICT 157-166
Water 48, 170
WIDER WORLD 167-182 & 50, 116, 118, 122, 128, 130, 132, 134, 136, 148, 150, 158, 160, 166 see also **HEALTH WORLDWIDE 101-110**
WORK 183-191 & 20, 28, 38, 66

Y

Young people 8, 10, 12, 26, 28, 30, 32, 36, 38, 58, 60, 62, 76, 82, 88, 112, 114, 120, 130, 176, 178, 186

Fact File 2012 © Carel Press, www.carelpress.com